A God Nearby

Three Medieval Views of
Immanence and Transcendence

Dr. Nathan D. Amerson

A God Nearby
Three Medieval Views of
Immanence and Transcendence

by Dr. Nathan D. Amerson

A publication of

The American Journal of
Biblical Theology
Illuminating God's Word

Hayesville, NC 28904
www.biblicaltheology.com

ISBN: 9798739872753 (Paperback)
ASIN: B091QFMQ8M (Amazon Kindle®)

Rights for publishing this book in other languages are contracted by the American Journal of Biblical Theology. The AJBT also provides publishing and technical assistance to international publishers dedicated to producing biblically based books in the languages of the world. For additional information, visit www.biblicaltheology.com or write to The American Journal of Biblical Theology, 41 Skid Strip Ln., Hayesville NC 28904 USA, or send an Email to editor@biblicaltheology.com.

Cover art: "Everything from Nothing". Copyright © 2021, Morgan Amerson.

Dedication

For Elaine, who never stopped supporting me.

"Am I only a God nearby," declares the Lord,
"and not a God far away?"

Jeremiah 23:23 (NIV)

TABLE OF CONTENTS

Chapter Five:
God Revealed in the Person of Christ

Chapter Six:
The Holy Spirit and God's Self-revelation within the Individual

Chapter Seven:

List of Abbreviations

CDH	*Cur Deus Homo*	Anselm
CoT	*Compendium of Theology*	Aquinas
Mono	*Monologion*	Anselm
Pros	*Proslogion*	Anselm
SCG	*Summa Contra Gentiles*	Aquinas
ST	*Summa Theologiae*	Aquinas

Acknowledgements

One cannot embark upon a work of this scale without an enormous amount of aid and support from a variety of sources. I am deeply grateful for the work of the authors I have used as sources in this exercise, most of whom I have never met yet without the research they have done and passed down to me I would be at a loss. I am the humble recipient of their labors and when we meet in heaven, I will be able at that time to fully express my gratitude.

Elaine, my wife of these many years, has been an unceasing champion of my labors, despite the many hours and days it has taken me away from family life. She never complained, and in fact encouraged me constantly, and for the many Saturdays spent at the library without any chastisement, I am forever grateful. Elaine, without you this small work would never have come to fruition.

To our best friends, Maija and Terry, I owe a debt for their continuous support and to Maija particularly for her careful reading of my manuscripts. Her critical eye helped me shape the paragraphs and chapters in a sensible manner, aided the transmission of my message, and pointed out several mistakes, typos, and grammatical issues. Without you both, I would have struggled to complete this work.

I am further grateful to several people who are not aware of the contribution they have made to this effort, yet from whom I have derived a great deal of moral support. To Dr. Greg

Ganssle, who directed the path of my dissertation early on and helped me to make sense of a project of this scale. To Dominic Sternhagen who helped me see some connections I make herein and with a wisdom beyond his years helped me chip away at the concepts I present in order to find the sculpture inside. To Anthony Costello, fellow theology student and fellow sufferer, who always encouraged, never let me quit, and also applied a critical reading to sections which benefitted greatly from his attention. In addition, to my advisor through the whole process, Dr. Leighton Flowers, for his support, input, and encouragement. I could not have accomplished this without you.

Finally to the librarians and staff of Mount Angel Seminary Library, I could never have taken on this project without the aid of your resources. The Library has become a second home.

I accept all responsibility for the material contained herein and any remaining errors in this manuscript are mine alone.

- *NDA*

Introduction

This work explores the writings of three great medieval theologians, all doctors of the church, and all enormously influential not only within their time but for centuries to come. Anselm of Canterbury, Bernard of Clairvaux, and Thomas Aquinas all held positions of significant sway within their monastic circles and their writings have continued to be points of reference, both for Catholic and Protestant theologians to this day. Simultaneously, a development of the twin themes of God's attributes of transcendence and immanence is an appropriate starting point not just for theology proper but for theology in general, and these three writers each contributed to an orthodox position which keeps a balanced position of these attributes in mind.

God is certainly transcendent from His creation by virtue of the fact that He created it. He exists outside our universe, outside of time, and in many ways outside our ability to understand. He exists for Himself alone and created the universe which relies upon Him alone for its sustainment. God set the laws of nature in motion, but continues to be active in the world today. He is a God of involvement with His creation, and most importantly with human beings, His highest creation. This personal interaction is His immanence to the world, and God Himself bridges the distance created by His wholly otherness, allowing Himself to be relatable and understandable. God created humankind with the faculty to know Him, to the extent that He permits, and to relate to Him in love. This in fact is the reason God chose to bring the First Persons into the world at all, out of a desire to relate to rational beings whom have been given real choice and genuine capacity to affect their own environment. Sin entered the world however and the pride of human beings became the undoing of the relationship God wished to have. Through the Incarnation and the Atonement, God orchestrated the means whereby He could be reunited in love with His creatures. To aid that reunion, He allowed His nature to be understandable, to a limited extent, by human beings, and so enabled relationship.

We will begin with God's transcendence and what the medieval theologians wrote on that topic. Utilizing Augustine as the precursor to the schoolmen and continuing through the three featured thinkers, this work unpacks medieval perspective on the transcendent nature of God. Then it develops how God makes Himself immanent and highlights the ways these three medievalists balance God's transcendence with His self-revelation through three avenues. These three are God's self-revelation in the Holy Scriptures, in the person of Jesus Christ, and in the indwelling person of His Holy Spirit in the life of the believer. Each of the three writers here encountered have unique perspective on these topics and impart wisdom and depth which continue to hold sway in theological circles today.

This work is additionally intended to demonstrate not only how three specific medieval theologians wrote and thought about theology proper within their time, but the continuing effect of their writings which span the gap of time and distance to the post-modern reader. Theology, over time, has developed in many ways as the major questions of the day are addressed by writers and thinkers within that particular context. At the same time, the core beliefs of the Christian faith have needed to be reexamined for each time in history for the simple reason that these core tenets are understood differently and applied differently in varying places, times, and cultures. Thus to revisit the writers of the past is to understand both what they were saying to their own time and how that message may be reapplied to the current time.

The value of historical theology is seen in understanding the concerns of both the time in history and the cultural context of the original writers, compared, contrasted, and re-applied to speak to a current perspective. This work attempts exactly that. In studying three great writers of medieval Europe and understanding their philosophy and their place in history as best we can, we will appreciate their theology as the foundational underpinnings of theology for the church at large within today's post-modern cultural framework. Anselm of Canterbury, Bernard of Clairvaux, and Thomas Aquinas, whose combined lifetimes spanned approximately two centuries, wrote for an audience that was scholastic, primarily monastic, and indelibly Roman Catholic. Using this starting point, this study embarks upon a conceptualization of these three thinkers as those who have lain the foundation of dogma for the Christian Church with effects continuing into the present.

Any study of historical theology is fraught with the difficulties associated with time and distance. Today's reader is simply not a member of the same culture, context, place in history, and environment as the medieval philosophers and so may find a connection with these great thinkers to be out of reach. It is vitally important to approach historical theology (and history in general) by reminding oneself that we do not fully grasp the fundamental properties of daily life within the historical context we are studying. We are outsiders, looking through a lens distorted by cultural, geographic, and technological distance from the era in which we have interest. Every attempt will be made in this work to avoid the pitfalls of the arrogance of modernity, where we may view persons from the Middle Ages as provincial, backward, and unaware of any larger context. Each person lives within their own time in history and so we begin with an introduction to the main characters whom we will be reviewing in depth to understand their theology.

Anselm of Canterbury (1033-1109) saw himself as first an academic, second a minister (more so to his brothers within the walls of the monastery than to the community), and a distant third as an administrator. He resisted those who recognized his leadership and desired for him to take a greater role in the administration of the monastery first at Bec and later at Canterbury.[1] Although in both cases he was the clear successor to Lanfranc, his mentor, this could be seen by everyone around him but himself. He doubted his abilities and frankly shunned the work of administration such as settling disputes, directing the daily activities of the monks, or worse yet dealing with lords and kings. He preferred instead the monk's cell, with its quiet and focus on transcribing, reading Scripture, writing, and meditation. As Archbishop of Canterbury, he learned over time how to adapt to his new roles, despite feeling they were thrust upon him undeservedly and certainly undesired. He found himself walking in new circles within the societal classes of his day, in the halls of kings and surrounded by knights, scribes, and governmental figures. This familiarization with the Norman feudal system is certainly a contributor to his understanding of the nature of the

---

[1] In modern day France and England respectively.

Atonement, a fact for which the *Doctor Magnificus* is criticized by post-modern theologians and historians. In many ways this is unfair, as any philosopher or theologian is certainly a product of his or her own time. No individual can distance themselves fully from their immediate culture nor should they be expected to do so. To imply the medieval thinkers were pre-critical then is in many ways an unfair designation as higher methods of critically thinking about the Scriptures had simply never been considered.[2] The three writers we address in this work were in fact ahead of their times, evidenced by the weight the Church has ascribed to their foundational teachings.

Around the beginning of the 12th century, some leaders within the monastic communities of France and the Low Countries began to express concerns stemming from a perceived trend among Benedictines, who had come to emphasize scholasticism for itself over Church ministry to laity and the non-monastic community. In the year 1098, while Anselm was still Archbishop in Canterbury, a group of Benedictine monks led by Robert of Molesme (1027-1111) and Stephen Harding (1050-1134) founded an abbey in Citeaux, in Dijon in Eastern France. Called Cistercians (from *Cistercium*, the Latin rendering of Citeaux), these monks believed the Benedictine order had become distanced from the rule as initially laid down by St. Benedict in the 6th century and felt a correction was necessary. Particular value was placed upon the monks performing manual labor, an effort which had been essentially relegated to the immediate communities who cared for the monks who were so deeply engaged in writing and translation. While French Benedictines of the time had largely distanced themselves from society by withdrawing

---

[2] The medieval views of Scripture and those of each of our writers will be examined in depth in Chapter 5.

into the monasteries and were conducting the work which would form the foundation of the Scholastic movement in Europe, many Churchmen felt the Church's ministry and outreach to lay persons within the local community was being left unattended. By leaving the cloister and physically working to provide for themselves, these Cistercian monks naturally became more integrated members of their local communities, a nexus which had been understated under the previous influence of Lanfranc and Anselm.

Simultaneously, the translation of ancient documents, transcription of the classics and works of the day, and burgeoning libraries allowed the monasteries to become the centers of education for Western Europe. However, the audience for these growing libraries and the teachings of the monks were in fact the monks themselves. Few outside the monasteries knew Latin, so the monasteries in their dedication to both preserve and generate the knowledge of the day, inadvertently became an insular mechanism, promoting the self-development of a very small group of people. It was the Cistercians who first endorsed a greater interaction between the monasteries and the surrounding communities, revived manual labor conducted by the monks themselves, and instituted the role of the itinerant friar who traveled about and ministered within the local community. Owing to an increased attractiveness of monastery life to the average citizen, coupled with increased social integration and burgeoning wealth as landholders, the Cistercian order met with great success and grew to over 500 religious houses by the year 1300, some as geographically removed as Wales, Scotland, Bohemia, and Castile. The success of the Cistercians set the stage for the mendicant orders to arise and fill an increasingly visible gap of ministry to the lay person of the community. [3]

Bernard of Clairvaux (1090-1153) was a man who came to prominence at this moment when reformation within the Church was becoming an issue of importance. At the age of 20, he joined the monastery at Citeaux in 1110, and rose to prominence within the order owing to his studiousness, devotion to prayer, adherence to the rule of St. Benedict, and natural intellect. Bernard was commissioned as the abbot of Clairvaux and went on to found numerous sister houses. He was a preacher foremost and is best known for his *Commentaries on the Song of Songs*. The exposition of this book is his life's work, but he was also famous in his own time for calming schism in the Church, setting up and taking down kings and popes, preaching a Crusade and recovering from its failure, establishing a new order of knights, and accomplishing all this while throughout his life suffering from poor health. Certainly the Church benefited from Bernard's Benedictine application of neo-Platonic thought, drawn from Augustine and applied within the contemporaneous context of monastic society, which contributed to development of doctrine.

Concern for proper monastic life and the relationship of the clergy to society began with Citeaux yet continued into the following century. Two movements arose almost simultaneously at the beginning of the 13th century to address the concern within the Church that the religious needs of lay people in the communities were being overlooked. Saint Francis of Assisi, burdened with the wellbeing of the community, founded an order in 1209 with rules based not on Augustine's Rules or those of Benedict but rather centered upon preaching and lay ministry. His

---

[3] Mendicant: those orders which were committed to poverty and sent preachers on visitation to various communities.

monks were not allowed to remain cloistered but were compelled to travel, preach, administer the sacraments, and in short, represent the Church outside the walls of the monastery. They could own nothing but their habit, were committed to poverty, begged for their daily needs, and traveled about on foot, becoming figures one would see in the street more so than the pulpit. In 1216, Saint Dominic also founded a movement of monks who were committed to many of the same principles and the two groups grew steadily to the point they were competitors for future members. Both Franciscans and Dominicans founded schools, preached in small parishes, provided for infant baptism, and performed last rites. In short, these mendicant orders became the face of the Church at large to the majority of lay people within local communities, persons who would never be invited to darken the door of a monastery yet still required administration of the sacraments and invited a pastoral ministry modeled on that of Jesus Himself. Particularly notable was a steady increase in the number of Franciscans and Dominicans (after 1228) attending the universities and viewing these centers of learning as the most favored places to build the religious and philosophical education they needed without being isolated in a monastery.

This rise of the universities was a major occurrence in the mid to late 12th century which brought needed variation to the educational landscape of Europe and enacted a series of changes which would forever affect the western world and the Church in particular. In 1100, the concept of the university was an idea for the future, therefore Anselm, Bernard, and the Benedictines of their time were concerned with the preservation of knowledge within the monasteries. Around the beginning of the 13th century, however, two universities were founded, the first in Bologna and closely followed by Paris. By the year 1500, this number had exploded to at least 62 across Europe, with a simultaneous expansion of a love of learning by more of the masses (although still a relatively small percentage of people were literate).[4] With the rapid expansion of the universities and subsequent expansion of the primary audience for learning beyond the Benedictine monk, the universities within the course of a single century displaced the monasteries as the primary centers of higher education. This in turn brought a change in focus toward classical philosophy, logic, and translation of Greek resources which started the European world upon a path of inevitable distance between the secular institutions of higher learning and those religious institutions which were committed to Church doctrine, history, and tradition.

The emergence of the universities is just one example of the many ways in which a study of medieval Europe provides valuable input to our postmodern worldview. The thinkers and leaders of the Middle Ages forged many of the concepts Western humanity has brought forward into postmodernity, although most post-moderns are usually oblivious to the effect of these people, places, and events of nearly 1000 years ago. Institutions such as modern banking, the university system, and current international trade law as well as developments such as nation-states and patriotism, ongoing tensions between Western and Muslim nations and states, the inevitable expansion into the "New World", and other principles which build the current post-modern climate owe their foundations to the Middle Ages. So too the explication of most of the foundational doctrines of the Catholic and Reformed Churches of today, as well as those of the less historically

---

[4] Miri Rubin and Walter Simon, eds, *The Cambridge History of Christianity: Christianity in Western Europe c. 1100-c.1500* (Cambridge: Cambridge University Press, 2009), map 2.

inclined modern Protestant non-denominational churches, was conceived in this time period.

Thus we arrive at the person of Thomas Aquinas (1225-74), cast in relief against this historical background in which he rose to prominence. A Dominican from North Italy, Thomas was educated first in Naples and later in the University of Paris (beginning in 1245), arguably the world's leading higher educational center of the time. Studying under Albert Magnus, the renowned instructor at Paris, Thomas' clear mind and devotion to study quickly brought him acclaim and success in this most challenging of academic settings, so much so that he was asked to stay on as a full-time professor. A key element of his teaching was a synthesis of Aristotelian rules of logic with a neoplatonist understanding of the Forms. He bridged the gap between the foundation laid by Augustine and Anselm (who both drew largely, although often indirectly, from Plato) and the reenergized interest, during his time, in Aristotle. This Aristotelian focus was a result of the re-introduction into Europe of translations of his work with commentary added by Arab writers, such as Avicenna and Averroes.[5] Thomas, faithful to his Dominican roots, never lost his reverence for the Holy Scriptures, despite his immersion in the increasingly secularized environment of the University of Paris. His theology was always soundly built upon the rock of the Word, and the philosophers with whom he interacted (Plato and Aristotle) were always required to confront the standard of God's highest form of self-revelation, the Scriptures. Using the rules of logic and the teachings of the greats, combined with a clear understanding of Scripture and Church dogmatics, Thomas strove to synchronize

---

[5] This migration of knowledge from Baghdad began due to wars between the emirs in the 12th century, and reached its height as scholars were escaping the sack of Baghdad by the Mongols in 1258.

church doctrine with the Greek philosophy of the neoplatonists and of Aristotle himself. He was driven to demonstrate the rational nature of Christianity and to systematize Church beliefs and in so doing his writings became the foundation of theology for the next eight centuries.

During Aquinas' lifetime, the universities began to enlarge their emphases to include additional fields of study. Earlier universities had focused their studies around grammar, dialectic, and rhetoric (or logic); the compatible disciplines of theology and philosophy formed the base of this *trivium*. By the time of Thomas' prime, not only had the number of universities expanded exponentially over the previous 40 years, but concurrently their concentrations had expanded to include additional subjects such as metaphysics, natural philosophy, medicine, alchemy, and mathematics.[6] Several of the leading universities also began to specialize in one discipline or another, thereby setting the stage for the decline of theology. No longer would she be the "Queen of Sciences", instead she was relegated to the field of humanities. This occurred simultaneous with an increasing emphasis on the natural sciences and mathematics which in their turn produced the Renaissance and with it a burgeoning Humanism.

The foundation laid by medieval theologians remains effectual into the present day, both in Catholic and Protestant theology, and the student who is blind to Christianity's debt to Anselm, Bernard, and Aquinas today, would be committing a grave error. The miscalculation of the post-modern theologian who does not recognize the benefit of studying theology in its historical context results in a misunderstanding of the foundational nature of

---

[6] Rubin and Simon, 403.

medieval dogmatics for the Church. Understood properly, historical theology builds upon doctrines drawn first from Scripture, further applied and expounded for a particular time and place, then reapplied in subsequent historical and cultural contexts till they come to the Church today for application to today's context. If it is true that history repeats itself, then failing to understand the application and development of theology in history will result in failing to apply the lessons learned from history into today's context. In understanding God's immanence and transcendence through a medieval lens, we will build a balanced perspective of these attributes of God's nature. In learning lessons from historical theology, we will further find application of these lessons in a postmodern world as we address the recurring complications which result from an overemphasis of one or the other.

CHAPTER ONE:
IMMANENCE AND TRANSCENDENCE

It may be argued from the outset that applying terminology and themes from systematic theology retroactively into a historical context, a context which did not employ such language at the time, may be a shaky foundation upon which to build. In exploring the themes of God's immanence and transcendence in this work as seen through the lens of the medievalists, we recognize the dangers inherent in applying a modern overlay to the words and writings of teachers from the 11th – 13th centuries. Rather than force the medievalists into a Procrustean theological framework, we instead seek to explore consistent themes which have been developed for the Church over time, even when those themes were not necessarily referenced in the same ways within their own time. Much as the New Testament nowhere employs the word "Trinity", it is obvious that Trinitarian themes are interwoven throughout its pages. Similarly, while the sacraments were not codified for the Church until the Council of Trent (mid-16th century), their importance to the Church and usage in the daily life of believers had already been central to religious life for many centuries. Likewise, the New Testament writers never had a concept of what today we would call "Christology", yet we may fittingly apply a model of Christological formula to our study of Scripture. In the same vein as these three examples, we will explore theological concepts which would later become schematized in systematic theology yet prior to the emergence of systematic theology as a field of study, have formed a basis for theologians across a variety of times in history.[7] Our three writers certainly understood and presented the concepts of God's immanence and transcendence for their particular times and audiences, and did so with purpose and in unique presentation. That they did so without necessarily utilizing terminology which was later developed within a context of systematic theology we accept and will attempt to use the same terminology they employed.

To open a discussion involving aspects of God's Nature, particularly His transcendence and immanence, we must address the ways in which God Himself chooses to interact with his created world.[8] Grenz and Olsen, the eminent historians, see a discussion of immanence and transcendence as the starting point for a historical view of Christian theology and weave the twin themes throughout their excellent overview *20th Century Theology: God and the World in a Transitional Age*. They note transcendence and immanence represent the primary ways in which God relates to the world and to humankind as a subset of creation. Speaking of His transcendence they write: "God is self-

---

[7] Without embarking upon a historical overview of systematic theology and various outlines within them of God's attributes of immanence and transcendence (a study which is quite well done by Grenz and Olsen), allow me to merely point the way to a few studies in both Protestant and Catholic theologies. Charles Hodge, *Systematic Theology, Vol. I* (Grand Rapids: Eerdman's, 1981), first appeared in print 1871. Karl Rahner, *Foundations of Christian Faith: An Introduction to the Idea of Christianity* (New York: The Seabury Press, 1978). Millard Erickson *Christian Theology* (Grand Rapids: Baker, 1983). Franz Josef Van Beeck, S.J., *God Encountered: A Contemporary Catholic Systematic Theology* (San Francisco: Harper and Row, 1988). Wolfhart Pannenberg, *Systematic Theology, Vol. I* (Grand Rapids: Eerdman's, 1988).

[8] Inclusion of this discussion here is designed to set the stage for considerations of these aspects of God's very nature, not to be indicative of how medievalists overtly saw God's transcendence and immanence. The views of the medievalists will be discussed in detail later, while this piece is designed to provide merely the backdrop for our exploration of Middle Age philosophy of religion.

sufficient apart from the world. God is above the universe and comes to the world from beyond."[9] Likewise speaking of God's immanence: "God is present to creation. The divine one is active within the universe, involved with the processes of the world and of human history."[10] These two aspects of the divine nature must be held in juxtaposition to one another, without the theologian swaying too far from a middle point between them.[11] The Bible clearly teaches that both descriptions of God are accurate so it is important to realize that to stray too far from a balance of the two aspects of God's nature will lead one into falsehood either way. A God who is only transcendent and not simultaneously immanent becomes unknowable and unrelatable. Too much emphasis on God's transcendence and one is left with Deism, which is to believe that God created the world but now exists somewhere outside the sphere of our daily lives. In a Deistic view, God is the Divine Creator who established the laws of nature, then stepped away to some other tasks and leaves His machine to carry on in His absence. Historically, this aspect of God's nature has been expressed by a variety of writers with a heavy emphasis toward the "otherness" of God, which has taken on various meanings depending on the author. For our three authors, God's transcendence is certainly emphasized in a medieval world where humankind is continually reminded of their inability to save themselves

---

[9] Stanley J. Grenz and Roger E. Olson, *20th Century Theology: God and the World in a Transitional Age* (Downer's Grove, Ill: Intervarsity Press, 1992), 11.

[10] Ibid.

[11] I appreciate Grudem's concise statement on these two attributes of God: "The Bible teaches that God is distinct from his creation. He is not part of it, for he has made it and rules over it. The term often used to say that God is much greater than creation is the word *transcendent*. Very simply, this means that God is 'far above' the creation in the sense that he is greater than the creation and he is independent of it. God is also very much involved in creation, for it is continually dependent on him for its existence and its functioning. The technical term used to speak of God's involvement in creation is the word *immanent*, meaning 'remaining in' creation." Wayne Grudem, *Systematic Theology* (Grand Rapids, MI: Zondervan, 1994), 267.

or even to choose what is right. Medieval theological writings are rife with separation of God from man, and emphasize a strong reliance upon the Church for absolution, the sacraments for right living, and the final administration of last rites to enter heaven upon one's death.

In counterbalance to transcendence, oversteering toward a position of God's immanence may result in earth worship, where God becomes so immanent to His creation that He loses His divinity and general revelation becomes God-in-itself. Another offshoot of an overemphasis on immanence is the belief that the revelation of God may only be truly known through what can be drawn from the human experience, which is the foundation of existentialism. In this way, God becomes so excessively revealed in His creature that man becomes God. Both positions are untenable. Therefore to strike the proper balance one must recognize that although humankind will never fully understand God's transcendence (that is, He is so far beyond our comprehension) or His immanence (that is, how can God reveal Himself in a intelligible way to frail and shattered man?), we can and must admit the truth of both sides of this coin which is the nature of God, and agree that they exist in a perfect cohesion. Grenz and Olsen again say: "Where such a balance is lacking, serious theological problems readily emerge. Hence an overemphasis on transcendence can lead to a theology that is irrelevant to the cultural context in which it seeks to speak, whereas an overemphasis on immanence can produce a theology held captive to a specific culture."[12] Indeed theology is only possible in that God's transcendent nature is made understandable by His self-limitation.

---

[12] Ibid, 12.

God's immanence can be further expressed in terms of God's knowability, of which Wayne Grudem writes: "If we are to know God at all, it is necessary that He reveal Himself to us."[13] And further: "It is not true to say that God cannot be understood, but it is true to say that He cannot be understood fully or exhaustively."[14] Similarly Thomas Merton, the great Catholic mystic writes: "In mystical experience, God is 'apprehended' as unknown. He is realized, 'sensed' in His immanence and transcendence. He becomes present not in a finite concept but in His infinite reality which overflows every analogical notion we can utter of Him."[15] By this Merton means humanity's experience of God must exist within the sphere of God's revelation of Himself, while also recognizing that God is only able to partially reveal Himself to humankind.

Where transcendence is God's "otherness" or separateness from the world, immanence is God's presence in the world. This presence is exhibited in a variety of ways, all of which may be expressed as forms of God's self-revelation. Without God limiting Himself and condescending to make Himself approachable in a way to flawed humankind, no person could begin to understand the nature of God in even a minute way. God must bring Himself to the world in a way that does not overwhelm the capacities of human reason and the senses, because humankind is unable to ascend to God's level. He is unapproachable in His very essence and so must reveal Himself to us if he is to be understood, even in a finite way.[16] Thus God's immanence to the world may be

---

[13] Wayne Grudem, *Systematic Theology* (Grand Rapids, MI: Zondervan Publishing House, 1992), 149.

[14] Ibid.

[15] Thomas Merton, *The Ascent to Truth* (San Diego: Harcourt Brace Jovanovich, 1981), 83.

[16] 1 Tim 6.16.

understood as His self-revelation. This will be explored through our medieval authors discussing God's revelation of Himself through three milieus: in the Holy Scriptures, in the Person of Christ, and finally through the Holy Spirit's presence within each individual.[17]

Augustine

Any approach to medieval philosophy must begin with a discussion of what had been preserved for these thinkers following the process of collapse of the Western Roman Empire and culminating with the death of the last true "Emperor of Rome" in 476.[18,19] Without embarking upon a dissertation of the historical landscape which led to the Middle Ages (a work which could and in fact has filled dozens of volumes), let it suffice to say the world of Western Europe was far different from that of the Roman Empire during her height. Dr. Maurice Keen writes: "Men [of the Middle Ages]...knew nothing of the commercial unity of the Roman empire, or its system of colonial administration. A common Latin culture and common religious beliefs, both inheritances of the past, brought men together, but martial

---

[17] Again, we recognize the application of a motif from systematic theology, yet understand these themes to have been inherent to Church teaching in the Middle Ages, albeit without being expressly portrayed in such particular language.

[18] After this time this title is only truly to be understood in an applied context for political purposes such as Charlemagne (800), or a religio/political context such as Sigismund of Hungary (1410). After 476, the term never again implied emperor over what was known as the Roman Empire, per se, except in the East.

[19] For the present work we accept Dr. Maurice Keen's designation of the Middle Ages as the time period bookended by the years 800 and 1449 respectively. This is a convenient designation which speaks to key events of the time, yet we recognize that the people living in those times had no distinct view of their time period as the "Middle Ages", a term which was coined far later during the Renaissance.

instinct and local and personal loyalties divided them still more deeply."[20]

While much had been lost since the times of the Romans, for philosophers and educated people some key works survived and became the core of learning for the time. In the waning years of the Roman Empire, many ancient works, carefully preserved up to that time, were lost, resulting in a lack of knowledge of the classics by western Europeans. While a paucity of the richness of learning during the heyday of the Roman Empire remained, it was enough for philosophers to establish a basis for education and learning. This culture would remain largely intact for the centuries leading up to the rediscovery of Aristotle with its commentary by the Arabs and the establishment of discussion of these works forming the basis of education in the universities. The 13th century witnessed both of these occurrences. Coupled with the loss of ancient works came the continental shift away from Greek as both the common language and that of learning and scholarship[21]. Latin became the language of the educated,

---

[20] Maurice Keen, *The Pelican History of Medieval Europe* (New York: Penguin Books, 1968), 24. He elaborates this point by stating: "In A.D. 800 when the Pope crowned Charlemagne emperor of Rome, western Europe stood dislocated by the decline of its economy since Roman times, by the Germanic invasions and the subsequent internecine feuds of the barbarians." All of these factors and others contributed to the making of the map of medieval Europe, politically, religiously, economically, and socially. This discussion, while fascinating, provides only the cultural and historical backdrop to the current work.

[21] Ferdinand Lot attributes this to the chaos of the time. "The cult of literature declined, or rather disappeared, in the towns of Gaul. In the midst of actions both good and bad, whilst the ferocity of nations and the fury of kings was breaking loose, when the Church was being attacked by heretics and defended by the faithful, and the Christian faith, burning in many hearts, died down in others, when religious establishments endowed by godly folk were despoiled by the impious, there was no grammarian, skilled in dialectic to be found who could retrace these events either in prose or in verse." Ferdinand Lot, *The End of the Ancient World and the Beginning of the Middle Ages*, trans. Philip and Mariette Leon (New York: Harper and Brothers, 1961), 371.

the language of business, and ultimately the language of religion and philosophy, resulting in learned men who could not read the classics in the original. Augustine (354-430) relied on translated portions of the Plato's *Timaeus*, and drew heavily from Latin authors such as Ovid, Cicero, Virgil, and Seneca for his understanding of classical Greek philosophy.[22] This continued to be the case into the 11th and 12th centuries, where Anselm had access to much the same resources as did Augustine nearly 800 years prior. A reliance on the teachings of Plato, translated by the Latin writers, was the norm so that, as Gilson points out: "Plato himself does not appear at all, but Platonism is everywhere."[23] So it is that the pervading philosophical influences coming out of the Western Roman Empire and continuing into the early centuries of the Middle Ages can be considered not true Platonism, but neoplatonism.[24] The primary advocate of neoplatonic thought for the Church was Augustine and Anselm was the first in medieval times who re-established neoplatonic thought patterns in discussion of dogma. Building upon Augustine, Anselm developed neoplatonic thought for the Church to initiate an age of scholasticism both within and outside the Church. This philosophical approach forms the basis of the present work and will be discussed in much detail in succeeding chapters.

---

[22] He relied upon Latin translations to such an extent that scholars today feel his study of the Latin classicists might compete with his emphasis upon Biblical reading. Indeed, Brenda Deen Schildgen at the 2019 LA Theology Conference in her plenary address entitled *Divine Providence: A Distorted Theology of History?* noted: "Augustine was as familiar with Virgil as with the Bible."

[23] Étienne Gilson, *History of Christian Philosophy in the Middle Ages* (New York: Random House, 1955), 144.

[24] For an excellent overview of Neoplatonism see Christian Wildberg, "Neoplatonism" in *The Stanford Encyclopedia of Philosophy* (Summer 2019 Edition), Edward N. Zalta (ed.), https://plato.stanford.edu/archives/sum2019/entries/neoplatonism.

Here we must embark upon an introduction to classical Greek philosophy with a focus upon those resources which were available to the medievalists. As has been stated above, beginning with Augustine and continuing into the 13th century, most writers of Western Europe had no direct access to the Greek philosophers in the original language, and so relied heavily on translated sections of original works and references to those works in some detail within Latin writers. Aristotle was hardly a point of reference until the late 12th century and early 13th century and so was little relied upon by the early medievalists. The first translations of the Arabic commentaries of Avicenna and Averroes and others, discovered during the early Crusades, were not available in Latin until Gerard of Cremona (d. 1187) and William of Moerbeke (ca. 1220-1286).[25] Thus where Anselm and Bernard had no access to Aristotle, by the time of Aquinas, Aristotle was being taught in the universities.[26] Because of this, Marenbon sees the rediscovery of Aristotle in Europe as the break point between "Early" middle ages and the later "Scholastic" or "High" middles ages, in the year 1200.[27]

For Anselm and the neoplatonists (who would not have used that term but rather referred to themselves simply as "Platonists"), several key understandings must be held in view. First is a concept of ideals, which Plato termed the Forms. Everything in this world is merely reminiscent of some ideal thing that exists in a higher plane of reality. For every chair made by man, there is a single highest form of

---

[25] Edward Grant, *God and Reason in the Middle Ages* (Cambridge: Cambridge University Press, 2001), 86. For more on this: F. C. Copleston, *Medieval Philosophy* (New York: Harper and Row, 1952).

[26] Jon Marenbon, "The Emergence of Medieval Latin Philosophy" in *The Cambridge History of Medieval Philosophy*, Robert Pasnau, ed. (Cambridge: Cambridge University Press, 2010), 38.

[27] Ibid.

the concept of "chair" which exists outside humanity's sphere of reach but is ontologically real nonetheless. Secondly, every action that occurs on the earth and in the realm of man's understanding is derived from a single source or cause. Christian Wildberg notes: "Neoplatonic philosophy is a strict form of principle-monism that strives to understand everything on the basis of a single cause that they considered divine, and indiscriminately referred to as 'the First', 'the One', or 'the Good.'"[28] Further, while one may learn about various aspects of the world, thereby increasing in understanding, true belief only comes about from being persuaded that all things which are visible to us in this world are but poor representations of the ultimate of those things which exist in the Forms. Julia Annas writes: "In the *Timaeus*, the Forms are presented in a very general way, as implied by our recognition of the differences between knowledge and true belief."[29] In referencing the Forms and the fact they are not entirely understandable because they exist in the realm of the gods, *Timaeus* says this: "If understanding and true belief are to different kinds, then absolutely there are these things 'by themselves', forms that are not perceivable by us, only thinkable."[30] Thus all things perceptible to human beings (including thought life, more on this later), flow from the ideal of those things which exists in the ether, the understanding of which requires trues belief, and all things in our world flow from the source of the ideals

---

[28] Christian Wildberg. "Neoplatonism." *The Stanford Encyclopedia of Philosophy* (Summer 2019 Edition).
https://plato.stanford.edu/archives/sum2019/entries/neoplatonism.

[29] Julia Annas, *Plato: A Very Short Introduction* (Oxford: Oxford University Press, 2003), 84. She goes on to clarify: "In the *Timaeus* itself Forms function as patterns for the Craftsman as he makes our world. Things in our world – species and kinds of thing, the four primary elements – are embodied in matter and spatially situated…and, crucially, they 'come to be', whereas Forms 'are, without coming to be.'"

[30] Quoted in Annas, 85, with her translation.

who is the highest Good, the First, and the Craftsman. One begins to understand the value for Augustine and others who saw many similarities between Christian belief and secular philosophy within a neoplatonist context.

St. Augustine, writing in Latin and in the 5th century, is the first of the neoplatonist Christian philosophers and may rightly be considered the bedrock of medieval philosophy. From the beginning of Christianity differences of opinion had led to great schisms in doctrine and belief and these perceptions of doctrine formed the basis of argumentation for the Patriarchs. Development of Christian dogmatics took place during the first six centuries of the Christian faith, such that by the time of Anselm these issues had been fairly cemented for the Church of the western world.[31] However for the early church writers and thinkers, the issues of Christ's nature and the Scriptures to be included in the canon became key aspects of dispute, and these writings in turn forged the beliefs of the Church. Through a series of councils, the Church determined which beliefs would be accepted as doctrine and which would be rejected, leading to the firm establishment of orthodoxy and heresy by the community at large. By determining which books should be included in the canon of Scripture (through the councils of Nicaea and others), Pope Damasus I was able to commission a new version of the Bible. This resulted in Jerome's Vulgate which became the officially accepted version of the Bible for the Catholic Church and remained so from the early 5th century until 1979. While Augustine did not have access to this work as a complete volume of Scripture, the Vulgate was the Bible

---

[31] It is interesting to note, however, the key aspects of Christian belief, it seems, are never completely settled. The value of historical theology is seen in uncovering the reasons why dogmatic differences were important for varying periods of history, how writers contemporary to those times discussed these dogmas, and what the Church as a whole drew from them for the development and establishment of those aspects of firm belief and faith. Undoubtedly this forms the foundation of research for the current writer.

of Anselm, Bernard, Thomas, and virtually every other writer and thinker of the medieval period and continuing into the Reformation.

In addition to establishing the canon of Scripture, the Patriarchs founded (again through a series of Church councils) the orthodox beliefs for the Church, although that process was fraught with dissention. The great writers of the early centuries of Christianity established the norms of belief for the community at large, and denied those beliefs which they felt were not in concord with the teachings of Scripture. Irenaeus (130-202) wrote to establish the concept of the Trinity and to balance viewpoints which held Christ was either God or man and could not be both. Clement of Alexandria (c. 150-215) and others countered Marcionism, which taught that the God of the Old Testament and that of the New Testament were two different Gods, one evil and blood-thirsty, the other loving and forgiving. Origen (184-253), opposed Docetism, a view which isolated Jesus' true self to his spirit form and taught His human body was merely an illusion. Athanasius (296-373) campaigned against Arianism, which held that Christ was created by the Father and was therefore inferior to Him. Against this backdrop of schism and heresy, Augustine (354-430) comes to the forefront in establishing Christian doctrine which would become the cornerstone of dogmatics for the Church.

For Augustine, Platonic thought forms his basis for defense of the Christian religion. Heavily influenced by Plotinus (204-270), the founder of neoplatonism, Augustine embarked upon the self-imposed task of understanding "the end of all human striving – union with a transcendent God" and from there to establish Christian belief utilizing the terminology of secular philosophy.[32] Jeremy Livermore writes: "Augustine

---

[32] Mary T. Clark, *Augustine* (London: Geoffrey Chapman, 1994), 6.

indubitably wanted to make a connection between Platonism and Christianity because he knew that besides the flesh and the internal debates within the Catholic Church the wisdom of the world was the most powerful & (sic) compelling force to fight against."[33] Gilson states that for Augustine the object of philosophy is happiness.[34] Happiness is found through true belief, and true belief is informed by the concept that the highest Form of happiness is found in relation to God, who is the Source of all things. Joseph Lienhard differs somewhat with this view, and feels while friendship with God is an important category of medieval theology (especially in Aquinas), it is to be found in Augustine only in trace elements.[35] Thus for Lienhard, Augustine's view of relating to God is focused more upon God's gift of grace which allows reinstatement for the believer into right status with God, rather than God desiring our happiness. This is underscored by Donald Burt who states: "For Augustine the central tragedy of being human just now is alienation – a state of being fractured in which we are separated from ourselves, each other, and the infinite God."[36] Mary Clark feels the starting point for understanding Augustine is his teaching on "free choice in relation to the larger liberty that comes from loving God."[37] She goes further to state Augustine was engaged in a "quest for wisdom, and in that quest he opened his mind to philosophic reason and to the authority that calls

---

[33] Jeremy Livermore, "Augustine", https://apologetics.com. Accessed 06 July 2019.

[34] Etienne Gilson, *The Christian Philosophy of Saint Augustine*, trans. L.EM. Lynch (New York: Random House, 1960), 3.

[35] Joseph T. Lienhard, "Friendship with God, Friendship in God: Traces in St. Augustine" in *Augustine: Mystic and Mystagogue,* Frederick Van Fleteren, Joseph C. Schnaubelt, and Joseph Reino, eds. (New York: Peter Lang Publishing, 1994), 208.

[36] Donald X. Burt. "Friendship and the State" in *Augustine: Presbyter Factus Sum,* Joseph T. Lienhard, Earl C. Muller, and Roland J. Teske, eds. (New York: Peter Lang Publishing, 1993), 249.

[37] Mary T. Clark, *Augustine: Philosopher of Freedom* (New York: Desclee Co., 1958), 1.

for faith."[38] All of these perspectives tie together various foci within Augustine and point clearly to his interaction with neo-Platonic thought, where the relation of man to the Divine essence is the most important aspect of our understanding. Augustine however branched out from these pagan viewpoints in tying our relationship with God to the Divine will in making such a relationship possible.

Transcendence

Augustine references God as "unspeakable", that is, no words of men can express His nature and His excellence beyond the world.[39] He also states that God condescends to make Himself known by man's understanding and ability and is composed of a "nature supreme in excellence and eternal in existence."[40] Augustine, it must be remembered, was heavily influenced in his younger life by the beliefs of the Manicheans and in later life by neoplatonism. In discovering the Christian faith and in defending it, he continued to draw both comparison and contrast with these belief systems. Reminiscent of Platonism he writes: "The highest good, than which there is no higher, is God, and consequently He is unchangeable good, hence truly eternal and truly immortal."[41] God cannot be compared to pagan gods, in that He alone is the Form of the Good, and by His nature is higher and outside any representation of good in the world. The Christian God is higher than all pagan representations of gods and is higher than man, who is His creation. Augustine again states: "God is, therefore, above every measure of the creature, above every form, above every order, nor is He above by local spaces, but by ineffable and singular potency,

---

[38] Clark, *Augustine*, 8.
[39] Augustine, *On Christian Doctrine*, I.14.
[40] Ibid.
[41] Augustine, *The Nature of the Good*, ch. 1.

from whom is every measure, every form, every order."[42] God is certainly transcendent from the world because He made it and everything in it. He is above creation because everything we see was brought about by Himself. God is also immutable and eternal, unchanging because He is the highest good and has nothing, therefore, to attain, and eternal in that He is unaffected by the passage of time.[43] God is the Creator of all things including time.[44] In Clark's words: "As pure being, God is eternal with no before or after. Time is one of the creatures, which according to Scripture as Augustine reads it, had a beginning."[45] God is the source of all things and because God is good, everything He has created is therefore good. This argument is made in response to the natural evil argument of the Manicheans.

Anselm builds upon the foundation of Augustine when he speaks of God "creating and ordering the universal frame of the visible and the invisible creation."[46] In his neoplatonist considerations (as evidenced particularly in the *Monologion* and *Proslogion*), Anselm speaks to the necessity of God's existence, and notes: "He is the supreme good needing no other and is He whom all things have need of for their being and well-being."[47] Thus again we see God is the highest Form of the good, created humankind and exists outside of man's understanding, and is inaccessible except by revealing Himself in an understandable way to humankind. Visser and Williams warn that in Anselm words which may be used to describe the attributes of God may not in the same way be

---

[42] Ibid, ch. 3.

[43] Gilson, *Augustine*, 143.

[44] Clark, *Augustine*, 35

[45] Ibid.

[46] Anselm, *First Meditation: On the Dignity and the Woe of Man's Estate*, S:1.

[47] Anselm, *Pros*, Preface.

used to describe any attributes of the created order, as God exists in and for Himself. It is only through God's self-revelation in granting understanding that He becomes understandable.[48] Donald Hogg further amplifies this tension in Anselm's outline within the *Proslogion*, showing how the magnificent doctor draws the reader's attention first to God's immanence and then to God's transcendence in both cases by discussing God's nature in relation to man's conception and thought.[49] Anselm develops this contradistinction between God's perfection and the state of man, contrasting God's transcendent nature with the fallen and despicable state of humanity throughout all his writings. Benedicta Ward states: "Sin for Anselm was not a personal psychological apprehension of wrongdoing and guilt: it was theological truth about man in relation to God."[50] Anselm's picturesque and (seemingly to the postmodern observer) heavily exaggerated language describing his sin and man's fallen state is designed to craft in the minds of his readers the indelible portrait of man's distance from God and God's perfectly transcendent nature. Eileen Sweeney connects this deeply emotional and personal language in Anselm's prayers to the Confessions of Augustine, where Augustine describes his struggles leading to conversion in terms of weeping and tearing his clothes. She goes further to note: "Anselm's first task is to depict the relationship between addressor and addressee, abasing himself and elevating God and the saints."[51] Hogg considers this to be the language of sorrow, directing penitent believers "into the presence of God, so that

---

[48] Sandra Visser and Thomas Williams, *Anselm* (Oxford: Oxford University Press, 2009), 75 and ch.6.

[49] Donald Hogg, *Anselm of Canterbury: The Beauty of Theology* (Burlington, VT: Ashgate, 2004), 121 (footnote 50 to chapter 4).

[50] Benedicta Ward, *Anselm of Canterbury: His Life and Legacy* (London: Society for Promoting Christian Knowledge, 2009), 12.

[51] Eileen C. Sweeney, *Anselm of Canterbury and the Desire for the Word* (Washington, D.C: Catholic University of America Press, 2012), 15, 17.

together they may discover the beauty of His plan the glory of its fulfillment."[52] In this way Anselm shows the divine nature of God to be so separate from our place in the created order that humankind cannot even reach to God out of our lowliness without some assistance from the saints, for which he prays in the Meditations.

Where Anselm's primary view of God's transcendent nature is that of separation from man by His very nature, a separation which is impossible for humankind to bridge due to sin, Bernard of Clairvaux speaks of this separation in terms of God's right to receive the love of mankind. Human persons, being made in the image of God, naturally possess free will, an intellect, and a certain virtue which God has given them to love, to seek, and to cling to the Creator. In this way Bernard distances himself from the language of self-abasement, which is so prevalent in the meditations of Anselm, and to the contrary ascribes to humanity the position of being God's highest creation. Indeed in failing to recognize the place of human persons in creation, humankind "sinks into the likeness of lower creatures by not knowing that [he] has received a greater thing than they."[53] Still, this is not to say that Bernard ascribes any gift to man which is of his own doing, and rather must hold in juxtaposition an understanding of his position higher than the rest of creation and yet far lower than that of the Creator. He moves on from the above quotation to note: "We must by no means esteem ourselves to be less than God has made us. But with still greater care we must avoid that other ignorance which makes us attribute more to ourselves than we possess, which we do when we mistakenly impute to ourselves the

---

[52] Hogg, 32.
[53] Bernard of Clairvaux, *On the Love of God*, ch. 2.

gifts we may be conscious of."[54] Thus God the Creator is our Benefactor, and in creating humankind has offered us the gifts of being able to realize both His reality and our reliance upon Him. The responsibility of man is "in all things to render the glory which belongs to Him."[55] God holds a claim to our love, and it is the obligation of humankind to love God the Creator who has revealed Himself to some extent in the creation, and who is duly worthy of the love which we owe to Him. Further owing to God's sacrifice of Himself in His son for the redemption of humanity, we are indebted to this gift which allows us even to approach His presence. Bernard elaborates upon this debt by saying: "If I owe my whole self to my Creator, what do I not owe to my Redeemer, and to such a Redeemer!"[56]

Both Anselm and Bernard explore the interlocked concepts of grace and free will and how those gifts of God are indicative of His holy nature. Anselm explores free will in a context of rectitude (Latin *rectitudo,* best translated as uprightness or right standing), where although God in His transcendent nature is all-powerful, He does not impose that omnipotence upon the free will of humankind which He has bestowed.[57] God desires humanity to be free to choose to worship Him, and did not create automatons who are forced (like the angels after free will had been taken from them) by their very nature to worship Him. God desired communion, however, that communion is broken by humanity's choice to sin,

---

[54] Ibid.

[55] Ibid.

[56] Ibid, ch. 5.

[57] Tsevreni ties this to a notion of correctness or truth, where humankind's proper standing which is restored to them results in "fulfillment of the norms of reason." Magdalini Tsevreni, "A Systematic Reading of *De Libertate Arbitrii*: The Ideas of Freedom and the Will of Saint Anselm," in *A Review of Medieval Studies*, 2 (2014), 61-78.

which again for Anselm is failing to give to God what one ought. Initially God provided for both free will and *rectitudo* which allowed the first created beings to freely commune with Him in the Garden. However, when humankind chose to fail to give to God what they owed Him, *rectitudo* was divested from choice, resulting a fallen nature for humankind which inclined them to sin. In this way God is separated from humanity by His transcendence and *rectitudo* is restored only when humanity wills what God wants them to do. For Anselm, the ability to will so is (after the fall) only granted through an impartation of God's grace, which necessitated the Incarnation and sacrifice of Christ.[58] It is important here to note that for Anselm humankind cannot overcome God's transcendence and come to Him. That restoration of humanity to God's presence requires *rectitudo*, which is only available to humanity through the Incarnation and the impartation of grace through the sacraments.

Bernard touches upon this subject of grace and free will with a more personal and less academic style than does Anselm. Of this discussion, William Watkins in his introduction to Bernard's *On Grace and Free Will* states: "There is about it the fragrance of mystical theology; not the mystical theology of the esoteric, but that of the simple Christian living in the world."[59] Salvation for Bernard is contingent upon human persons choosing to undo Adam's original choice by accepting God's free gift of grace, which humanity cannot attain for themselves. As in Anselm's description, God's transcendence is bridged by God's grace, and humanity in

---

[58] This is an overview of three works of Anselm: *Cur Deus Homo, On Free will,* and *On the Virgin Conception and Original Sin.* Also see a good discussion on the development of medieval views of free will in Tobias Hoffman, "Freedom Without Choice: Medieval Theories of the Essence of Freedom," in *The Cambridge Companion to Medieval Ethics*, ed. Thomas Williams (Cambridge: Cambridge University Press, 2019), 2.

[59] In *Saint Bernard of Clairvaux: Collection*, (Aeterna Press, 2016).

reaching out to accept that grace by an act of the will "is said to co-operate with the grace which worketh salvation, when the free will consenteth, that is to say, is saved; for to consent is to be saved."[60] However, human persons are unable to choose to reach out to God without an infusion of His grace for "...freedom of will is yet in certain fashion held captive."[61] Humanity is given free choice through our will yet owing to original sin we are unable to choose what is right.[62] Bernard elaborates: "It is in virtue of free choice that we will, it is in virtue of grace that we will what is good."[63] Bernard shows that an infusion of grace is necessary first for humanity to choose to accept salvation and is imparted through the work of Christ who restored to humankind the image of God in which we were originally made. Indeed it is Christ's free choice which imbued men with the grace to choose to accept God's salvation.[64]

Having explored notions of God's transcendence in Anselm and Bernard, we turn to those concepts in Thomas Aquinas. Aquinas is incredibly systematic in his theological development and employs a measured and calculated methodology in his *Summas*. In his approach to theology proper he describes both what God is and what He is not. Thomas believes that while God is transcendent and outside man's comprehension, He is understandable for two reasons:

---

[60] *Concerning Grace and Free Will*, ch. 1.

[61] Ibid, ch 6.

[62] Hoffman again states: "Bernard adopts Augustine and Anselm's view that freedom of decision is not the power to choose between good and evil. But Bernard in point of fact disconnects freedom of decision from the good: the bad angels have freedom of decision even though they cannot choose good. What makes the will free is not that it acts well, but merely that it acts willingly." Hoffman, *Freedom*, 3.

[63] Ibid.

[64] Ibid, ch. 11. Much more on this topic will be presented in Chapter 6 of the present work.

first because He created humankind with the faculty of reason to think about God in reasonable and practical ways and second because God reveals Himself in a comprehensible manner. That is not to imply that God may be known fully, only partially due to His transcendent nature. Of Aquinas' position on knowing God Davies writes: "In saying that we cannot know what God is, therefore, he is chiefly denying that God can be defined or placed in a class. He means that our knowledge of God is not comparable to that which a scientist has of things."[65] Thus Thomas is clear in his position on God's incredible distance from fallen humanity and the fact that He exists on a plane which is in many ways outside of our understanding. Still he does not place knowledge of God on a level beyond approaching. Davies again: "Aquinas does not mean us to believe that we have no knowledge of God. At the same time, however, he thinks that the nature of God is, in a sense, incomprehensible to us – that God defies our power of understanding."[66] O'Meara refers to this balance of God's knowability and unknowability as Thomas speaking of the "unknown but present God."[67]

Aquinas held a unique view of God that was shaped by his philosophy; unique in that he was the first to synthesize elements of neoplatonism with the writings of Aristotle which had recently been rediscovered in Europe.[68] Aquinas saw God as a pure being and pure essence, existing on a plane beyond human comprehension. Etienne Gilson expands upon this correlation between Aristotelian thought and

[65] Brian Davies, *The Thought of Thomas Aquinas* (Oxford: Oxford University Press, 1992), 41.

[66] Ibid.

[67] Thomas F. O'Meara, *Thomas Aquinas: Theologian* (Notre Dame: University of Notre Dame Press, 1997), 90.

[68] James Doig, "Aquinas and Aristotle" in Brian Davies and Eleonore Stump, eds., *The Oxford Handbook of Aquinas* (Oxford: Oxford University Press, 2012).

Thomist theology. He writes: "The pure being that Aquinas the philosopher encountered at the end of metaphysics, Aquinas the theologian also met in scripture, no longer as the conclusion of a rational argument, but as a revelation from God himself to the human race to be accepted by faith."[69] For the study of the present work, no other statement could so well encapsulate the thought of Aquinas. In one area particularly Aquinas highlights God's transcendent nature and that is in his development of the Divine Ideas. Drawing upon the Forms of Plato, Aquinas shows that highest ideal of any concept exists in the mind of God. Tethering that concept to Aristotelian philosophy Aquinas shows the Divine Ideas to be causes of ideas in humanity, so humankind's reason is seen as being formed in the image of God in that His ideas are the first causes of human thought. Excellent work has been done on this topic, particularly by Doolan and Sternhagen, to whom we will turn for further exposition later.[70]

Particularly in the *Summas*, Thomas defines God's nature by describing the attributes of God. In this way the systematic theologies of the postmodern era continue to draw upon the great medievalist. Aquinas describes God's infinity, His immutability, His eternity, and His simplicity, all of which are ways of getting one's hands on understanding God despite His transcendence.[71] Thus God's transcendence is

---

[69] Etienne Gilson, *Thomism: The Philosophy of Thomas Aquinas*, trans. Laurence K. Shook and Armand Maurer (Toronto: Pontifical Institute of Medieval Studies, 2002), 95.

[70] Gregory T. Doolan, *Aquinas on the Divine Ideas as Exemplar Causes* (Washington, D.C.: Catholic University Press, 2008) and Dominic Sternhagen, "The Divine Ideas in North American Thomism" (Licentiate Dissertation, Pontifical Athenaeum Regina Apostolorum, Sep 2014).

[71] Brian Leftow outlines these nicely in "God's Impassability, Immutability, and Eternality" in Brian Davies and Eleonore Stump, eds., *The Oxford Handbook of Aquinas* (Oxford: Oxford University Press, 2012).

manifest is in His perfections.[72] He goes further to describe God in terms of His activities such as His providence, justice, mercy, power, and beatitude which speak to His immanence to the world. God is acting within His creation even as He exists without it and beyond it. Despite these efforts to communicate the nature of God, the distance between the human reason and truly grasping God's nature is such that God remains essentially unknowable. Healy states Thomas assumes and draws upon an established Church doctrine "that God the Creator is transcendent, ontologically separate from what God created out of nothing."[73]

God's Self-revelation in the Holy Scriptures

The interaction of the medievalists with the Bible is quite different than that of Augustine, primarily in that Anselm, Bernard, and Thomas referenced the Latin Vulgate where Augustine did not have access to this work in its entirety in his time.[74] Not only that, the hermeneutic approach of our three doctors is quite different in the 11th, 12th, and 13th centuries than was Augustine's approach to Holy Scripture in the 5th. Where the ancients have been said to have a "pre-critical" approach to Scripture, this may be somewhat unfair as the resources available to today's theologian are so vastly outside the realm of thinking of the ancient philosophers as

---

[72] What in systematic theology today we would term God's "incommunicable attributes".

[73] Nicholas M. Healy, *Thomas Aquinas: Theologian of the Christian Life* (Burlington, VT: Ashgate, 2003), 59.

[74] Jerome and Augustine were contemporaries and Augustine certainly was aware of the ongoing translation effort made by Jerome during his lifetime. Augustine seems to have drawn from some of these translations while largely relying upon his own and those of the Greek fathers. La Bonnardiere makes a compelling argument for Augustine's use of Jerome's translations in a variety of his writings. Anne Marie La Bonnardiere, "Did Augustine Use Jerome's Vulgate?" in Pamela Bright, ed., *Augustine and the Bible* (Notre Dame, IN: University of Notre Dame Press, 1999).

to present a situation of incomparability.[75] This must be kept in mind by the postmodern as we interact with the medievalists. Origen in the 3rd century first laid out a prescribed method of reading Scripture to gain its meaning in a two-fold manner. First is the "inferential historical sense" where the meaning of the text is adequately conveyed in its surface transmission through language, and second is a "spiritual interpretation" of the text in which a deeper meaning exists which is only revealed to the reader when an allegorical reading is brought to the surface language.[76] Augustine built upon this when he explained that the plainly revealed things in Scripture should be first attended to, that is those passages from which are drawn the matters of faith and life. Then when one has become familiar with the plain meaning of Scripture the reader may branch out to those more obscure passages, continuing to draw parallels back to those places in Scripture which hold a plain or obvious surface meaning.[77] Augustine downplays the error of extracting from the text a meaning which is unintended by the original author if the intent of the reader is to build up love among members of the Church. Thus a mistaken interpretation is to be corrected but gently as the intent of the reader was righteous. However, Augustine does show that errors in interpretation may compound, leading the reader further down an incorrect path which can end in heterodoxy. A final thought from Augustine which may come as a surprise to the modern disciple of Scripture is that it is possible for a person to become so saturated with faith, hope, and love that they no longer require the Scriptures for themselves but only for instructing others.[78] Shortly after the

---

[75] Rhyne Putnam, *In Defense of Doctrine: Evangelicalism, Theology, and Scripture* (Minneapolis: Fortress Press, 2015), 61.

[76] Origen, *De Principiis*; IV, 12-13.

[77] *On Christian Doctrine*; II, 9.14.

[78] *On Christian Doctrine*; I, 9.

death of Augustine, Vincent of Lerins (d. 445) established a standard for interpretation of Scripture which was held for the most part into the Middle Ages. He stated: "We hold to that which has been believed everywhere, always, and by all people," a rule which is completely impractical although it appears on the surface to be grounded in piety.[79] This statement draws heavily upon the authority and tradition of the Church, but in practice is indefensible as no belief held by anyone in the Church throughout time fits into the category of being so undisputed.

Anselm's approach to Scripture may be summed up in saying that its every word may be used in prayer back to God and its authority as the basis for Christian life cannot be questioned. His reference to Scripture as the "word of God" in *De Concordia* aligns perfectly with his view, consistent throughout his writings, that Scripture is the final reference for every point he makes. God speaks in holy writ and in so doing a seed of salvation is transmitted to the reader.[80] God Himself is thus revealed in the recorded words and in His grace and offer of salvation show Himself to man. Further, as man is designed in God's image, his reason is an extension of God's design. Human beings are called to use their reason yet simultaneously make it subject to the word of God. God's divine communication to humankind in the Bible represents an authority over man's reason and nothing which may seem reasonable yet is denied by Scripture may be accepted. On the flip side of this coin, if a reasonable consideration arises which is in no way contradicted by Scripture, that concept may be allowed to flourish. Of this combined effect of Scripture and rationality, Evans notes: "Anselm's doctrine of

---

[79] "*Quod ubique, quod semper, quod ab omnibus creditum est.*" Quoted from Putnam, 63.

[80] Anselm, *De Concordia*, ch. 6.

Scripture and reason is of a piece with his theory of a *continuous revelation* in the community of the Church."[81]

Humanity, for Anselm, is separated from God by sin, which he defines variously as stealing from God, or as failing to give to God what is owed. Sin is revealed in the heart of an individual by one's conscience, and by the witness of Scripture. Thus the seeds of God's grace, which proceed from His very person through the writings of the prophets become evidence of God's presence in the life of the believer. Man's separation from God can only be overcome by God's grace which He condescends to offer from His great and lofty position above that of any human being. While man's reason is a representation of God in creation, reason alone cannot find its way to God without God's act of grace in the life of the believer. If God did not condescend to show Himself in an understandable way, there would be no method for humankind to overcome its own failures and if God did not reveal Himself in the Holy Scriptures, humanity is unable to even believe God exists. God is further revealed by His grace in igniting the spark of faith which allows us to believe first, then to seek to understand. Sweeney says of this: "The larger anthropology which Anselm is working out is one in which human beings are both responsible for their fall (because of free will) and unable to redeem themselves (hence in need of grace)."[82] Finally Anselm shows, for humanity to receive God's grace, to even look up from their despicable condition, requires the intercession of Mary and the saints on behalf of the believer. R. W. Southern, Anselm's eminent biographer, refers to this combination of "penitential self-abasement"

---

[81] Evans, *Anselm*, 41. Emphasis mine.
[82] Sweeney, 181. Parentheses original.

38

and "the approach to a final state of contemplation through meditation" as the "foundation of Anselm's spiritual life."[83]

Bernard was a devotee of the Word, steeped and marinated in its contents. For him the whole Bible was meat and bread, sustaining his learning and devotion to God. Cristiani states:

> Concerning the Psalms, which were the principal content of the Divine Office of each day, Bernard used the charming expression: "the delightful rumination of the Psalms." He had them always in mind. He "ruminated" over them to extract their fullest savor. And what he did for the Psalms he evidently did for the whole of Scripture, so that he soon knew the entire Bible by heart....The Bible was imprinted deep in his soul, like an open book, each of whose passages he knew very well.[84]

Bernard's attention to the Scripture is best seen in analysis of his writings where allusion to Biblical passages or direct quotation may be seen occurring as frequently as one reference for every two lines.[85] This saturation with the Word is best seen in Bernard's many sermons, which utilize the format of a *homily* or conversation, and include volumes of references to the Scriptures, to the extent the great preacher seems not to know where his own words end and those of Holy writ begin. It was Abelard's use of Scripture which first raised Bernard's ire, for the Cistercian felt Abelard was careless in his exegetical approach and bent the Word to his

---

[83] R. W. Southern, *St. Anselm: A Portrait in a Landscape* (Cambridge: Cambridge University Press, 1990), 104.

[84] Leon Cristiani, *St. Bernard of Clairvaux* (Boston: Daughters of St. Paul, 1977), 50.

[85] Anthony Lane, *Bernard of Clairvaux: Theologian of the Cross* (Collegeville, MN: Liturgical Press, 2013), 54.

own interpretation. Bernard also made different use of Scripture for different audiences, where in his sermons, especially those preached to large lay audiences on the feast days, we see a liberal sprinkling of reference to the Bible. Simultaneously in his deeper reflections which were designed for his monastic brothers and assumed a deeper knowledge of religion as a vocation, Bernard gets deeply into the meaning behind the text. This is best seen in his *Commentary on the Song of Songs*, where he references in his introduction two other books, Ecclesiastes and Proverbs, as two loaves of bread, drawing upon St. Paul's presentation of "solid food" to those for whom the deeper things of God are understandable.

Bernard also employs a freedom in interpreting allegory, where in his Commentary on the Song of Songs he draws principles for the relationship of the Church (and its members) to God from this love poem, which describes the rapture between a man and woman. The postmodern reader might object to Bernard's use of allegory which is applied without apology and stated as fact. However, by the time of the Middle Ages it was largely believed (contrary in some ways to Augustine's teaching) that most if not all of Scripture involved interpreting those parts which present deeper meaning beyond face value.[86] Bernard provides this meaning and its application to the Church in his Sermons and Commentary on the Song of Songs, and does so for the edification of his students and listeners.[87] In similar ways he approaches the Annunciation, Mary's reception of this message, and the Nativity, in his series of sermons delivered for Advent. These delightful addresses turn the attention of

---

[86] Evans, *Bernard of Clairvaux*, 60.
[87] Ibid, 68-69.

the hearer to God, to His perfect son Jesus, and to Mary, the greatest intercessor for the souls of believers.

Finally for Bernard, the Scriptures are God's words without doubt, His direct messaging to humanity. He frequently refers to passages from the Bible as "the words of God" and notes in a sermon: "These, my brethren, are the words of God Himself, and it is not lawful for us to doubt them."[88] Evans here notes: "It could be argued that all language 'properly' speaks of God, for reference to God can never be a secondary matter. It could, on the other hand, be argued that no human language can 'properly' speak of God but only His own word."[89] The Bible is God's very words, recorded for us, and as such are the most relatable form of representing Himself for posterity. Thus the Scripture is God's revelation of Himself in an understandable way to humankind, it is His very own words, and as such is authoritative for the life of the believer.

For Thomas Aquinas God has made Himself knowable, that is to say as knowable as He can when limited by revealing His glory to an imperfect species. Healy states: "But beyond our evident feebleness, Thomas also believes that we need the apostolic witness to teach us the limits of human reason even at its best. Scripture shows us that God makes known to us in what is other than God."[90] God has provided the Scriptures as a witness to himself and those Scriptures must be read from a position of the first principles of theology and Scripture's necessity both philosophically and theologically.[91] In his works of theology, Thomas employs the words of Scripture far less often than the previous two medievalists we have here reviewed, largely due to the fact

---

[88] Sermon LXXXIV, *On Seeking God.*

[89] Evans, *Bernard of Clairvaux*, 70.

[90] Healy, *Thomas Aquinas*, 59.

[91] Ibid, 35-36.

that he is drawing heavily upon philosophical language to show the existence of God, His creative power, and God's causative effects within the world. However His reference to Scripture is seen throughout, in his discussions on the Trinity, the divine person of Christ, the angels, and humanity's responsibility in avoiding sin and extolling the virtues. In reference to the holy Scriptures as God's divine self-revelation, Thomas states: "Even as regards those truths about God which human reason could have discovered, it was necessary that man should be taught by a *divine revelation*, because the truth about God such as reason could discover, would only be known to a few."[92] He goes further to state: "[I]n order that the salvation of men might be brought about more fitly and more surely, it was necessary that they should be taught *divine truths by divine revelation*."[93] In the theological world of Aquinas, the Bible was the bedrock or faith, or argument, and of proposition, forming the foundation of discourse. Davies writes: "For Aquinas, as for the other professors at Paris in his day, the Bible was the word of God, and, therefore, something in the light of which other teaching was to be judged...In his view, access to revelation is given in the words of canonical Scripture, and especially in the teaching of Christ contained there."[94] Thus Scripture is always viewed by Aquinas as authoritative and as God's revelation of Himself, immanent into the world.

It is in Thomas' commentaries on Scripture that his devotion to these documents becomes most vibrantly evident. God's revelation of Himself in the Person of Christ is, for Aquinas, the greatest contribution of the Bible, but its parts form a

---

[92] *Summa Theologiae*, I-I.1.1. Emphasis mine
[93] Ibid, emphases mine.
[94] Davies, *Thought*, 12.

sum of authority for the life of the believer. The Scriptures outline God's attributes and His work in the world and within humanity. Because the Scriptures are God's divine self-revelation, they show all aspects of Christianity, from the sacraments to the virtues, to natural and divine law, and all others. Sacred doctrine is based upon the revealed nature of God in Scripture couple with men's reason and ability to understand the way in which God has chosen to reveal Himself in the recorded word. Davies outlines Aquinas' view that because God could not reveal Himself fully to humankind and because humanity's reason is flawed, the Bible makes use of analogy in talking about God.[95] Additionally the Scriptures require the reader to have faith and belief as an *a priori* consideration in that God is not truly knowable. By speaking to what God is, and what God does, and what God is not, the Bible allows the reader a glimpse into the person of God Himself, a tangible revelation of that which is transcendent.[96]

God Revealed in the Person of Christ

For all three of our writers, the person of Christ is a central theme, not merely because He represents God's personal agency in the created world, but because He represents God Himself in bodily form. The import of this self-revelation of God in Jesus Christ cannot be overstated as it is a consistent theme throughout the writings of the Middle Ages. That God revealed Himself to those eyewitnesses and recorders of the life of Christ demonstrates God's willingness to condescend to humanity, to make Himself understandable, to speak personally and verbally into the world, and to initiate,

---

[95] Davies, *Thought*, 70.

[96] Martin Pickave, "Human Knowledge" in Brian Davies and Eleonore Stump, eds., *The Oxford Handbook of Aquinas* (Oxford: Oxford University Press, 2012).

through His death, that process by which mankind may be reunited to God Himself.

The mystery of Christ is best outlined in Anselm's *Cur Deus Homo,* translated as "Why God Became Man" or more literally "Why a God-man?" By no means the only work in which Anselm explores the divinity and humanity of Jesus, this volume stands on its own as a depiction of Anselm's basis of belief in the Trinity and in God's immanent and personal self-revelation of Himself to the world. Anselm introduces this work by asking: "By what logic or necessity did God become man, and by his death, as we believe and profess, restore life to the world, when he could have done this through the agency of some other person, angelic or human, or simply by willing it?"[97] He goes out of his way to affirm clearly the separate yet combined natures, one divine and one human, and as Evans writes: "When God became man, God was not diminished; instead, man was exalted."[98] Further the return of mankind into right standing with God was accomplished through Christ's purposeful choice and willingness to sacrifice Himself for us. Evans refers to this as His obedience which every rational creature owes to God and emphasizes that Christ was not compelled to suffer and die, in fact could not have been or the effect of His sacrifice of a sinless life in place of man's sinfulness would have been undone.[99] Visser and Williams indicate a reliance upon Chalcedonian Christology forms the basis for *Cur Deus Homo,* and the post-modern reader must understand Anselm's emphasis on the intertwined aspects of Christ's work (soteriology) and Christ's nature (Christology). For Anselm the former dictates the necessity of the latter.[100] Southern tells us that two themes

---

[97] Anselm, *Cur Deus Homo,* 1.1.
[98] Evans, *Anselm,* 75.
[99] Ibid.
[100] Visser and Williams, *Anselm,* 213.

are particularly outlined in *Cur Deus Homo*, first "there cannot be the slightest deficiency or imbalance either in God's nature, or God's creation" and "everything that God does follows a perfect order that is not only perfect in its rationality, but also supremely beautiful."[101] Hogg beautifully represents the basis of our current research in stating: "In the *Cur Deus Homo*, we see the plan of redemption unfold in all its beauty, harmony and fittingness as the transcendent God recreates and reorders sinful humanity through the immanence of the incarnation."[102]

Anselm also emphasizes the two natures of Christ in the *Epistola De Incarnatione Verbi* (Letter on the Incarnation of the Word) and gets into a deep discussion regarding the nature of the Trinity in the *Monologion*. Sweeney states that in *On the Incarnation of the Word,* Anselm explains "the orthodox view as a unity of human *nature* with the *person* of the Son of God, one person with two natures."[103] This is an important *inclusio*, forming a basis of doctrine and rationality for Anselm, which we will explore in greater depth in this chapter. Visser and Williams feel the primary purpose of *On the Incarnation of the Word* is to refute a heretic, thus Anselm relies on Church authority and rationality to explore the difference in nature and person.[104] He demonstrates the difference between the word of God as an utterance and the Word of God revealed in a person, Jesus Christ. Slotemaker restates the distinction of persons in *On the Incarnation of the Word* in terms of distinguishing between "divine relations" and "divine substance".[105] Hogg indicates *On the*

---

[101] Southern, *St. Anselm*, 181.

[102] Hogg, *Beauty*, 157.

[103] Sweeney, *Anselm*, 267. Emphases original.

[104] Visser and Williams, *Anselm*, footnote 4 in chapter 9.

[105] John T. Slotemaker, "The Development of Anselm's Trinitarian Theology: The Origins of a Late Medieval Debate" in Giles E. M. Gaspar and Ian Logan, eds.,

Incarnation of the Word is linked with *Cur Deus Homo* through Anselm's restatement of a basic truth which relies upon the human being's grasp of three concepts. First man must understand the basic elements of truth, then must receive illumination by God's self-revelation, and finally understanding and illumination are brought to their highest realities through experience. Simultaneously, experience alone is not enough if not rooted in belief.[106]

Bernard speaks of the person of Christ in beautifully stirring language, bringing the reader to a point of deep personal interaction with this most unique and august person. In his sermons for Advent, Bernard crafts a portrait of Christ as a babe, yet marvelously and incredibly still God even in that form, losing none of the power of God yet clothing Himself in a bodily form with which humankind may relate. He says: "Attend and see how Omnipotence is ruled, Wisdom instructed, Power sustained; the God Who rejoices the angels is become a Babe at the breast; He Who consoles the afflicted lies weeping in a manger."[107] For Bernard the purpose of God becoming Man was to win back for Himself that which was lost, namely the love of humankind. Only through God's perfect sacrifice could humanity be placed back into a position of being able to interact with God, for man's decision in the Garden to be independent of God through sin had resulted in a condition of being unable to love God. God had created human beings for that purpose and human beings had fallen into a position of being unable to fulfill their created purpose. Only through the sacrifice of God Himself could a spark of love be reignited within humankind and only then could we begin to fulfill our created destiny which is

---

Saint Anselm of Canterbury and his Legacy (Durham: Durham University, 2012), 209.

[106] Hogg, *Beauty*, 158.

[107] Homily II, *The Mission of the Angel*, from Sermons of Saint Bernard on Advent and Christmas.

loving and being loved by God. Bernard brings his listeners to relate with the immanence of God in Christ who holds both divine and human natures simultaneously and shows how considering these two natures brings one back into a condition of loving God. Not only must mankind love God in a human or fleshly way, but mankind is called to love God in a spiritual way, a way which is only imparted to humanity by the sacrifice of the immanent God. Cristiani states the purpose of Bernard's preaching: "We must rise from 'carnal' love, or *sentiment*, to '*spiritual*' love, that is to say, the prayer of union, as the mystical writers of a later time were to call it."[108]

Another aspect of Bernard's Christology is the restoration of the image of God within humanity. Through original sin, humankind had lost not only the ability to love God as we were created to do, we had also defaced the image of God. Having been created to physically represent God's likeness in the world, humanity had spoiled that likeness and "encrusted [it] with the filth of sin."[109] Christ in taking the form of man retained His divine nature and subjected man's ability to choose, which had resulted disastrously in establishing a sin nature for all humankind, to the power of God within Him. This subjection of His human will to the divine nature and His sacrifice for all humankind resulted in humanity now having the ability returned to us to choose to love God. Of this Anthony Lane states: "In all manner of life Christ strove against sin, by word and example, but it is by his Cross and resurrection that the battle is won."[110] Gilson shows the power of spiritual love or pure love burns out of human beings all that is not from the Creator, only love of

---

[108] Cristiani, *St. Bernard*, 52, emphases original.

[109] *Concerning Grace and Free Will*, Chapter X.

[110] Lane, *Bernard of Clairvaux*, 142.

God can return us to our natural state of union with God.[111] Thus the image of God is returned to His creation when we choose in this life to love God with a spiritual love and when in the end of time we are raptured to be with Him in eternal likeness of glory.

Thomas in his careful way spends a great deal of attention devoted to the person of Christ. This central figure is treated at length in several of Thomas' great works, to include the *Compendium of Theology*, *Contra Errores Graecorum*, and *Summa Theologiae*. The reason for this is of course the fact that every age of theology in history has struggled with the concept of the coexistence of divinity and humanity in the person of Christ, and some have strayed too far from a perfect balance of the two and into error and opposition to church dogma. In the *Compendium* after spending some pages discussing the nature of divinity and the Trinity as jointly possessing such divinity, Thomas turns to a dissertation on the personhood of Christ with these words: "[W]e shall do well to inquire first how the human race fell into sin, so that we may understand more clearly how men are freed from their sins through Christ's humanity."[112] Thus it is seen from Aquinas that the balance of Christ's divine and human natures simultaneously and in totality of being represent the transcendence and immanence of God Himself in relation to the world.

Aquinas certainly see the complexity of understanding the person of Christ in simultaneous divine and human terms, recognizing that this must be accepted as an article of faith and cannot be seen as a scientifically provable point. Gorman shows: "Instead, it is revealed by God through

---

[111] Etienne Gilson. *The Mystical Theology of St. Bernard*, trans. A.H.C. Downes (London: Sheed and Ward, 1955), 142.

[112] *CoT*, ch. 185.

Scripture as authoritatively interpreted by the Church."[113] Aquinas speaks of Christ as one person. This is important because it shows how in Christ the fully divine and fully human natures reside simultaneously. That Christ carried both natures in the world is most important when we consider that without the divine nature and human capacity for reason and free will, Christ could not have carried out the work of reconciliation which His death on the cross brought about. Davies states: "To say that Christ must be acknowledged in two natures is to say that one may truly affirm of Christ what is properly affirmed of God and human beings."[114] Gorman goes on to state that Christ's human and mental powers allow him to perform true human acts.[115] Jesus possessed both the divine perfections and human weaknesses, yet never exercised those weaknesses in the body, thereby becoming the perfect sacrifice. For Aquinas, reconciliation (*rectitudo*) means a mending or repairing of what was broken, necessary in that the perfect harmony of God and humankind in creation was fractured, thereby leaving humanity with a diminished reflection of God's image. God in His perfection, as the ideal of all things, could not allow His highest created order to so poorly reflect the *imago dei,* thus He establishes the means by which this may be repaired, the only means by which this is possible. That is not to say that the incarnation was necessary for atonement in the same sense that Anselm proposes, for Aquinas is loath to limit God's power in any way. Rather the Incarnation is the most fitting means God could have

---

[113] Michael Gorman, "Incarnation" in *The Oxford Handbook of Aquinas* Brian Davies and Eleonore Stump, eds. (Oxford: Oxford University Press, 2012), 429.

[114] Davies, *Thought*, 301.

[115] Gorman, "Incarnation," 431.

proposed for this reunion of a damaged creation with its Creator.[116]

Another aspect of Thomistic Christology which must be considered is the establishment of the Church as the ongoing representation of God in the world. This permanent immanence of God's character and person into the world was established by the God-man who imparted grace into His disciples for the purpose of establishing God's church for all time. Dauphinais and Levering show that Thomas projects Christ as the fulfillment of the Old Testament in that the "name" of God would dwell in the Temple, that is to say the prayers emanating from the holy place become the embodiment of God. Likewise the liturgy of the church and prayers to God, Mary, and the saints are the embodiment of the nature God in the world today. Dauphinais and Levering point out: "Thus, the emphasis in the Old Testament on the Temple as the place of true worship is connected by the New Testament with Christ's perfect worship (on the cross) and human beings' participation in Christ's perfect worship as members of his Mystical Body."[117] Aquinas alleges that Christ as the head of the church may be retroactively applied even to those who believed and existed before His bodily ministry.

---

[116] Davies, *Thought*, 323. For a further development of this concept in Aquinas particularly see Mark K. Spencer, "Perceiving the Image of God in the Whole Human Person," in *The St. Anselm Journal*, 13:2 (2018): 1-18.

[117] Michael Dauphinais and Matthew Levering, *Knowing the Love of Christ: An Introduction to the Theology of St. Thomas Aquinas* (Notre Dame, IN: University of Notre Dame, 2002), 99. Parentheses and capitals original.

The Holy Spirit and God's Self-revelation within the individual

Anselm, in his argumentation against the differences in beliefs held by those Eastern believers whom he referred to as "the Greeks", outlines the nature of the Trinity in clear discourse, referencing in many places the certain divinity and personality of the Holy Spirit. Using language which is influenced by Platonism and in particular his reliance upon *Timaeus*, Anselm argues that while the Holy Spirit is of one substance with God, He proceeds from the Son and the Father for the purpose of revealing God to humankind. The work of the Holy Spirit, who is God revealed to humanity, is to teach truth to humanity, Truth which is in fact a personal revelation of the nature of God to us. Anselm shows us: "By the Holy Spirit the hearts of men are taught things which they knew neither from themselves not from any other creature."[118] The Holy Spirit teaches truth to minds which are distant from God by virtue of His transcendence. Only through the Holy Spirit working in the life of the believer can right reason be restored once humanity has chosen the way of sin. This sin, which separates humankind from God as a result of the desecration of the *imago Dei* within humanity, prevents human reason from reaching its pure intended purpose which is to understand Truth and to understand God.[119] Additionally, where truth is revealed in Scripture, that truth is made fertile and effective in our reason through the work of the Holy Spirit.[120] Thus the Holy Spirit works in humankind to reveal and explain God's truth and indeed God Himself in the life and mind of the believer.

---

[118] *On the Virgin Conception and Original Sin*, 11.

[119] This outline is a summary derived primarily from Anselm's argument against the Eastern Church beliefs in *On the Procession of the Holy Spirit*.

[120] *De Concordia*, 6.

Bernard speaks of the Holy Spirit as being revealed to be God Himself. There can be no doubt as to the divinity of the Holy Spirit when he references Jesus Christ as "the Mediator between God and man...who with the Father and the Holy Spirit reigns *as God* forever."[121] Evans considers the nature of the Trinity in exploring various notions of unity, such as in marriage two become one flesh and soul and sprit are unified in the human being. She goes on to show that for Bernard: "only in the Godhead is the unity that of a single substance."[122] Building upon his analogous description of the Holy Spirit as the kiss which is passed between the bride and groom in the Song of Songs, Bernard indicates the Holy Spirit proceeds from the Son and reveals God the Father as well. He states: "He [the Son] reveals himself therefore, and the Father as well, to whom it pleases Him. And it is certain that he makes this revelation through the kiss, that is, through the Holy Spirit."[123] Thus God reveals Himself in the world through the Holy Spirit in an immanent and intimate way. Just as humankind is called to love God, and was created for that fact, although sin damaged our ability to even do so, the love between the bride and groom (analogously of God and the Church) is evidenced by a kiss, and this kiss for Bernard is the Holy Spirit. Bernard goes further so say the Holy Spirit is given as a gift to humanity, a gift which itself reveals God to us. God chose first to reveal Himself in the world through humankind, His highest creation. When that created order fell from its perfect state into one of being unable to fulfill the role for which it was created, God further revealed Himself in the world in the person of Christ, the perfect God-man. Finally, God leaves evidence of Himself in the person of the Holy Spirit who

---

[121] Sermon 2 on the Song of Songs, *Various Meanings of the Kiss*, 9. Emphasis mine.

[122] Evans, *Bernard*, 75.

[123] Sermon 8 on the Song of Songs, *The Holy Spirit: The Kiss on the Mouth*, 4.

represents the love of God for Humanity and the love which is returned to God by his creation. "It is by giving the Spirit, through whom he [God] reveals, that he shows us himself; he reveals in the gift, his gift is in the revealing."[124] Gilson shows how for Bernard the Holy Spirit is God and is in humankind as a gift in that the Holy Spirit is one and the same with God, and becomes love for God in humanity.[125] We are restored then to our intended purpose by the power of the Holy Spirit uniquely applied within each believer.

Not only does the Holy Spirit bring humanity back into alignment with creation's intended purpose, but He also continually reveals God in the world and in the heart of the believer. This immanent aspect of God in the life of the believer is given for several purposes. Without adding undue prioritization, one purpose is that by invoking the Holy Spirit in our prayers this third person of the Godhead reveals God's very name and presence in our lives.[126] Another is that the words of Scripture were given to us "under the Holy Spirit's guidance chiefly for the instruction of people who have succumbed to their own corrupt passions."[127] In this statement we see a two-fold immanence of God to the world in the instruction given in Scripture and in the person of the Holy Spirit who Himself instructs us. Additionally for Bernard the Holy Spirit is active and speaks into our lives, speaks of truths and lights the way for our continued discovery of our role in loving God. The Holy Spirit infuses the believer with the love and light of God and is effused out of the believer into others through the performance of good works. The work of the Holy Spirit in the life of the believer is an underlying theme throughout Bernard's commentary

---

[124] Ibid, 5.

[125] Gilson, *Mystical Theology*, 211.

[126] Sermon 14 on the Song of Songs, *The Church of Christ and the Jews*, 8.

[127] Sermon 15 on the Song of Songs, *Meaning of the Number '7' and the Qualities of True Confession*, 1.

and sermons on the Song of Songs, a book upon which he relies throughout his writings and preserved spoken word.

Aquinas shows first (in the *Summa Theologiae*) how the term "Holy Spirit" when divided into isolated terms may in fact be truly applied to all members of the Trinity, who are in themselves holy and spirit by nature. However the Holy Spirit may also be, and if fact *must* be, considered the third and unique person of the Godhead, although understood as proceeding from the Son and the Father as the Son proceeds from the Father. Both are unique persons in themselves, are full members of the Godhead, which is one, and Aquinas points to these persons as proceeding from the Father in different expressions: the Son representing the intellect of God as "Word" and the Spirit showing the Love of God.[128] Thus the Spirit is the Love of the Father for the Son, and is further seen as the ongoing Love of the Father for His church. The gift of the Holy Spirit represents God's personhood and His affection for His creation in a unique and interesting expression of immanence. Davies puts this so well when he says: "[But] Aquinas also believes that the 'immanent Trinity' is the 'economic Trinity.' For he thinks that God both acts in the world and is present in it."[129]

Humankind is not able to turn to God except by two motions which are initiated by God Himself. The reason is turned to God by the procession of the Son into the world, who materializes and embodies a relatable aspect of God's nature in the world. While Aquinas never removes the responsibility of the believer to live as God wills in the world, the reason of a human being is brought to faith by an infusion of God. This is presented first in the Man Jesus Christ and furthered by the transformative work of God in the life the believer who

---

[128] *ST*, I.a.36. Also see Davies, *Thought*, 206.
[129] Davies, *Thought*, 207.

willingly accepts the work of faith within the reason.[130] Secondly humankind is enabled to love God by the presence of the third person of the Trinity. The Holy Spirit represents God's love in the life of the believer, first toward God, enabling good works, and second toward his or her fellow human being.[131] In this way the immanent nature of God is seen in the world and the life of the believer through the Son bringing one's reason to a position of faith, and the Holy Spirit bringing one's actions in line with godly virtue.

For Aquinas, in distinction to Bernard and Anselm who simply did not approach a discussion of the Holy Spirit in the same manner, God through the Holy Spirit gives gifts to men. In this way the immanent relationship which the Divine One is able to have with fallen humankind is both allowed by the personhood of the Holy Spirit and fostered by the gifts the Holy Spirit brings. These gifts allow humanity to evidence the *imago dei*, which would ordinarily be impossible without the redeeming work of Christ and the ongoing presence of God in the lives of believers through the Holy Spirt. Andrew Pinsent draws an excellent series of distinctions between Aquinas' view of the virtues (an Aristotelian term), the gifts of the Spirit, and the further fruits of the Spirit.[132] The virtues are employed by Aquinas in a somewhat different manner than in Aristotle. Aquinas does not espouse the Aristotelian concept that we can acquire the virtues by good deeds, rather that the virtues must be infused in the believer by God. The moral life demonstrates the *imago dei*, yet relies upon an infusion of grace, an acceptance of the gifts of the Holy Spirit, and a living out of the results of those gifts. In

---

[130] Healy, *Thomas Aquinas*, 125.

[131] John Baptist Ku, *God the Father in the Theology of St. Thomas Aquinas* (New York: Peter Lang, 2013), 263.

[132] Andrew Pinsent, "The Gifts and Fruits of the Holy Spirit" in *The Oxford Handbook of Aquinas* Brian Davies and Eleonore Stump, eds. (Oxford: Oxford University Press, 2012).

turn, this moral lifestyle is reliant upon and empowered by the fruits of the Holy Spirit. In this way God is immanent to the world and His presence is demonstrated through the good deeds of human beings living out the virtues of God Himself, infused not acquired, as evidenced by the fruit of the Spirit.[133]

---

[133] Dauphinais and Levering, *Knowing*, 55.

CHAPTER TWO:
AUGUSTINE

The contributions of the Early Church Fathers

During the early centuries of the Church, the nature of God was a hotly debated topic, and a church-wide understanding of the importance of having a balanced perspective of His co-equal attributes of immanence and transcendence was brought to the forefront. Though disputed by the early Fathers, such topics as the nature of God, the divinity of His Son, and the written works which would be considered the canon of Scripture were ultimately decided upon by the majority of church leaders and accepted as dogma. While the present work is not a development of the doctrines of the church by the early Fathers (indeed so much has been written on this topic as to render an overview almost impossible), the stage must be set for the writings of the one man whose influence upon medieval theology cannot be overstated: Augustine.

The Early Church Fathers leading up to Augustine wrote for their particular times and places in history in the centuries immediately following the life and work of Christ on earth. Remembering the balance which must be struck in understanding the transcendence and immanence of God, we explore these writers with that balance in mind. Irenaeus (130? – 202) was a disciple of Polycarp, who was in turn the last disciple of the Apostle John. This connection to those who had personally walked with Christ was important to him, and he wrote to counter heresies which were already springing up in the Early Church. In speaking of God's transcendence, a theme which was interwoven throughout much of the early church writings, he says: "Since God is vast, and the Architect of the world, and omnipotent, He created things that reach to the immensity...in order that the entire fullness of those things which have been produced might come into being, although they had no previous existence."[134] Thus does this earliest writer of the post-Apostle church speak of God's potency and divine nature, clearly outlining the fact that He exists beyond human understanding.[135] He goes on to write: "For this is the property of the working of God, not merely to proceed to the infinitude of the understanding, or even to overpass our powers of mind, reason and speech, time and place, and every age; but also to go beyond substance, and fullness or perfection."[136] This is a common theme among the Fathers, who, as we shall see, developed a concept of God which exhibits His transcendent nature.

Clement of Alexandria (c. 150 – c. 215) was so knowledgeable of both traditional Greek philosophy and mythology as well as the words of Holy Scripture that he could write the most convincing argument against heathen worship of the time. After establishing the nature of the Greek gods and their worship, using terminology familiar to his audience, he shows how the God of the Bible far exceeds the corrupted nature of the heathen gods. Turning from mythology to the

---

[134] Irenaeus, *Fragments from the Lost Writings of Irenaeus* in Phillip Schaff, ed., *The Complete Works of the Church Fathers* (Kindle edition, Public domain), Fragment 6. All subsequent quotations from the early church fathers will be found in Schaff's work.

[135] Hall shows the reason for this in Irenaeus is that although humankind had been created precisely to understand God and be able to interact with Him, humanity's current condition of being unable to reach to God was a natural result of the sin of Adam, the cosmic man. Stuart G. Hall, *Doctrine and Practice in the Early Church* (London: SCPK, 1991), 65.

[136] Irenaeus, Fragment 6.

Scriptures he concludes: "Behold God's greatness, and be filled with amazement. Let us worship Him...."[137] This for Clement is the natural conclusion, where in demonstrating the weaknesses of the heathen gods and the perfection of the true God he can only bring his audience to its knees in worship of the infinitude and mercy of God. He goes further to point out God's creation of humanity and the wonder and complexity of the human body. After asking: "Who liquefied the marrow? Or who solidified the bones?" he goes on to compare the miracle of the human frame to the miracle of God's reconciliation and asks: "Who bestowed righteousness? Who promised immortality?"[138] Clement answers his own questions with this statement: "The Maker of the universe alone; the Great Artist and Father has formed us, such a living image as man is."[139] This statement on transcendence was intended to speak to his audience of the unsurpassably of God's power, knowledge, and character, in contradistinction to the weak and diminished natures of the Greek gods.

While Clement wrote to counter heathen beliefs, Origen (c. 184 – c. 253), speaking to an audience composed of believers who differed in opinions, wrote to establish doctrine. Origen noted that God is not composed of a body as humans would understand it but rather is understood to be Spirit and further describes Him as "incomprehensible, and incapable of being measured."[140] He goes further to indicate man's inability to even reach an understanding of God due to our

---

[137] Clement of Alexandria, *Exhortation to the Heathen*, chapter 6.

[138] Ibid, chapter 10.

[139] Ibid.

[140] Origen, *De Principiis,* 1.1 *On God*. Hall expounds upon this by saying: "Origen held God to be transcendent in a manner combining Platonic and Aristotelian notions. God is pure spirit, without body or parts…Origen argues that God is pure mind and any similarity to creatures is in their rationality." Hall, *Doctrine and Practice*, 105.

weakness and the ontological separation of creation from Creator. He notes: "For whatever be the knowledge which we are able to obtain of God, either by perception of reflection, we must of necessity believe that He is by many degrees far better than what we perceive Him to be."[141] Origen elaborates this point in saying: "...we must of necessity hold that there is something exceptional and worthy of God which does not admit any comparison at all, not merely in things, but which cannot even be conceived by thought or discovered by perception."[142] Thus God is unattainable by the human mind, cannot be seen or fully understood, and exists on such a separate plane from humankind as to be unapproachable.

Athanasius (c. 296 – 373) begins his Statement of Faith with this concept: "We believe in one Unbegotten God, Father Almighty, maker of all things both visible and invisible, that *has His being from Himself*."[143] This indicates that God exists in and of Himself, for Himself alone, and speaks to His transcendent nature, referencing what would later be termed the "aseity" of God (from Latin *a se*, literally "from self"). In the introduction to his great work *Against the Heathen*, Athanasius points to the supremely transcendent nature of God, describing Him as a "Being beyond all substance and human discovery" and notes that human persons have no choice but to be "awe-struck as he contemplates that Providence which through the Word extends to the universe."[144]

In each of these early writers we see God's transcendent nature amplified, with varying intent and to differing audiences, but in no case do we see on overemphasis which is not counter balanced by a discussion of God's immanence.

---

[141] Ibid.

[142] Ibid, 1.2 *On Christ*.

[143] Athanasius, *Statement of Faith*, 1. Emphasis mine.

[144] Athanasius, *On the Incarnation of the Word,* 7.19.

We recall from our discussion in Chapter 2 that immanence may be understood to be God's revelation of Himself in an understandable way to the world. Athanasius speaks to this concept in stating that God is "revealed in the Universe", that is by His creation. In speaking to both the deity and humanity of Christ, Athanasius shows how humanity's limitations in sense and understanding are bridged by God's revelation of Himself in the form of Jesus Christ. Humans could interact with His physical body on earth during His life, yet He simultaneously acted out the divine nature, thus showing God's immanent presence on earth.[145] Additionally God is revealed in the creation, although not to such an extent that the created order becomes God-in-itself. In countering heathen earth worship, Athanasius shows the incompatibility of nature as god in that the same action may be found in nature to man's benefit and to man's harm. This concept shows nature itself to be not god but rather indicates the nature of God as "the Leader and Artificer of the Universe."[146] Further, Athanasius goes on to show that God may be known by the soul in humanity, for in creating an intellectual and immortal soul in humankind, God has revealed Himself in that way also.[147]

Working back through our discussion above, we find Origen refers to Christ as God's Wisdom "hypostatically existing" that is, being a corporeal demonstration of the incorporeal

---

[145] Athanasius here is writing to counter the Arian heretical doctrine which taught God's Son was the highest creation of God, rather than God Himself. God reveals Himself in the Son and in His earthly work, becoming immanent to the world, but the Son is God, not merely His best created work. Williams clarifies this nicely in saying: "What is emerging here [in Athanasius] is an argument for continuity of substance between Father and Son on the basis of a continuity or identity or "indiscernibility" of *action*. In creation and redemption, God does one thing, but does it in a pattern of interwoven self-revelation...." Emphases original. Rowan Williams, "Athanasius and the Arian Crisis," in *The First Christian Theologians*, ed. G.R. Evans (Malden, MA: Blackwell, 2004), 165.

[146] Athanasius, *Against the Heathen*, 1.29.

[147] Ibid, 2.34.

nature of God.[148] God's immanence to the world in the co-equally human and divine person of Christ in fact represents God's very Wisdom in bodily form. Further Christ as God the Son reveals God the Father in an understandable way to humankind, simultaneously representing in his human body the divine nature and presenting God to the rationale of humankind.[149] Origen goes on to point out God's revelation of Himself in Scripture and indicates that God must limit Himself to be understood by his fragile creation. Origen shows the reader: "For although no one is able to speak with certainty of God the Father, it is nevertheless possible for some knowledge of Him to be gained by means of the visible creation and the natural feelings of the human mind; and it is possible, moreover, for such knowledge to be confined from the sacred Scriptures."[150] In this one sentence, Origen beautifully sums up God's accommodation for the purpose of being understandable and approachable by a severely limited humanity.

Clement of Alexandria refers to Jesus Christ as "the husbandman of God...having bestowed on us the truly great, divine, and inalienable inheritance of the Father, deifying man by heavenly teaching, putting His laws into our mind, and writing them on our hearts."[151] Thus Christ tends the garden of the minds and hearts of humankind, bestowing a

---

[148] Origen, *De Principiis*, 1.2.2.

[149] Williams shows how in Origen Christ is the Logos and is one with God, and is the one spirit that has not fallen from its natural relationship with God the Father. "When God seeks to restore fallen humanity, he does so by allowing this spirit which is perfectly united with the Logos to take on flesh. Because of its unique relation to the flesh, it is not subject to the earthbound and self-centered desires and habits that imprison our spirits, and which require a lifelong ascetic monitoring." For Origen, Christ's life and death are the perfect self-gift to the Father resulting in restoration of the created order to its intended purpose. Williams, "Origen," in *The First Christian Theologians*, ed. G.R. Evans (Malden, MA: Blackwell, 2004), 139.

[150] Origen, *De Principiis*, 1.3.1.

[151] Clement, *Exhortation to the Heathen*, ch. 11.

relatable image of God through understandable laws. The human person's inherent rationality is both a gift from God and is intended to be how God reveals Himself to us. Christ's role on earth was in living to show God in a physical form to earthbound creatures and in dying to be the means by which humanity is restored to their intended position of relationship with God. His continuing ministry is to speak wisdom into the heart and mind of any person who would receive this evidence of God Himself in a rational manner. Our role is first to have faith in God, second to accept His self-limiting revelation rationally that we may understand Him more, and third we are called to be grateful. Clement exhorts the believer: "And though God needs nothing let us render to Him the grateful recompense of a thankful heart and of piety."[152] Hall points out that for Clement, faith is not "blind faith" or an irrational expression of humanity's desperation but rather is the first in a series of logical steps, humanity reaching beyond ourselves to the God who reveals Himself.[153] Further for Clement God is truly revealed in the words of Scripture for he refers to the voice coming from Scripture in a personal sense as "The Instructor." The Word is God revealed in wisdom and instruction for the reader. Scripture is understandable and is God's self-limiting witness to Himself that humankind may read and understand.[154] Sin is irrational; reading the Word and following it, resulting in piety and the glory of God, is in fact humankind's most rational response. Osborne clarifies: "Faith was the beginning, knowledge the way and love the end."[155]

---

[152] Ibid.

[153] Hall, *Doctrine and Practice*, 98.

[154] This concept is beautifully laid out in *The Paedagogus*, ch. 2.

[155] Eric Osborne, "Clement of Alexandria," in *The First Christian Theologians,* ed. G.R. Evans (Malden, MA: Blackwell, 2004), 129.

Irenaeus strikes the balance of immanence and transcendence as well in showing how the Holy Spirit reveals God to a weak and corrupted humanity, speaking to us in comprehensible ways that we may understand some of who God is. Humanity is given knowledge of the Creator by the Holy Spirit, the Holy Spirit allows us even to accept the grace of God through the sacrifice of Christ, and allows us to live in a way that bridges the distance between us and God Himself.[156] Fallen human beings "having been deprived of the Divine Spirit...fail to attain to the kingdom of heaven."[157] In this way humanity is restored to our intended positon in relation to God, first through the work of God in Christ, immanent to the world in a physical body, then through the ongoing work of the Holy Spirit, who is God Himself revealed in the heart and mind of humankind.[158] Osborne refers to this conceptually as humankind's participation with God, Christ becoming human that humans might become like Him, restored in their natures to their original relationship with God. He shows that for Irenaeus "Humans participate in God's truth through faith and reason", a concept which will translate very nicely into our later discussion of Anselm.[159]

Thus we see through the Fathers that most important leveling of the scales as it were, between recognizing God's transcendent nature as being beyond us, beyond the reach of our understanding, yet simultaneously God having shown

---

[156] Irenaeus, *Fragments*, fragment 27.

[157] Ibid, fragment 36.

[158] Kelly expounds upon Irenaeus' doctrine of redemption and ties it closely to a doctrine of Adam as an archetype of Christ. "The conclusion to which his argument leads is that humanity, who as we have seen was seminally present in Adam, has been given the opportunity of making a new start in Christ, the second Adam, the incorporation in His mystical body." J.N.D. Kelly, *Early Christian Doctrines* (New York: Harper Collins, 1978), 173.

[159] Eric Osborne, "Irenaeus of Lyons," in *The First Christian Theologians,* G.R. Evans, ed., 125.

some of Himself to us in a manner which is understandable and relatable. We will now see how the great Augustine wove these two themes in setting the stage for what would much later become the medieval theology we will explore in later chapters.

Augustine, Philosophy, and Transcendence

"*All* medieval theology is 'Augustinian', to a greater or lesser extent."[160] With this unequivocal statement Alister McGrath, the eminent church historian and theologian, begins a section of his work on the doctrine of justification. The foundation that is laid by this early theologian is so basic to the writings of Church thinkers who would follow as to require an overview of his contribution to the work at hand. While space does not permit an in-depth assessment of Augustinian theology as a whole, and indeed entire sections of the library are committed to him, we must at least draw back the curtain in addressing Augustine's presentation of the topics at hand, that is, God's immanence and transcendence.

Augustine's story is well known, and we will not dwell upon it here in depth. Born in North Africa in 354 to a devout Christian mother, Monica, and a pagan father, Augustine was well-educated from an early age. As a teen he departed from the way of life his mother had chosen for him and indulged in many of the worldly entertainments available to him, as would any other youth of any time. He found his way to Carthage where he was exposed to the teachings of the Manicheans, concepts which appealed to him and seemed to answer many of the difficult questions he was left with from his upbringing with his Christian mother. Later, while still a devotee of the Manicheans, Augustine traveled to Rome and

---

[160] Alister E. McGrath, *Iustitia Dei: A History of the Christian Doctrine of Justification* (Cambridge: Cambridge University Press, 2005), 24.

thence to Milan where he was exposed to the teachings of Plato, Plotinus, Cicero, and one Bishop Ambrose, an excellent rhetor and preacher of the Christian faith. It was in Milan that Augustine saw the weaknesses in Manicheism in light of neoplatonism, coupled with the convincing rhetoric of Ambrose, and he embarked upon a study of the works of the Apostle Paul. Upon experiencing a real conversion to Christianity at the age of 33, Augustine returned to Africa, making his way to Hippo Regius where he was made first assistant priest to Valerius, then successor and bishop of Hippo. Here he wrote most of his great works, engaged in debate, battled heretical beliefs, and mentored many young priests of the Church. He died in 430, engaged in prayer for his adopted city, which would succumb, after his death, to a Vandal siege.[161]

Augustine's genius is seen in his application of neoplatonic thought to defense of the Christian faith. As we noted in Chapter Two, he saw in the Christian God the highest expression of what is good and beautiful and wise and true. God, for Augustine, is the Form of these virtues and in representing the highest form which can only be poorly imitated on earth, God exists ontologically outside the ability of humankind to relate or truly understand. In his introduction to a small philosophical work written later in life and drawing upon his experience as a follower of Mani he writes that God is the highest good, He is unchangeable, He is omnipotent, and He made all things out of that which was previously non-existent. Augustine exposits: "Therefore every spirit, though subject to change, and every corporeal entity, is from God, and all this, having been made, is nature."[162] Because God is the highest good, the Form of

---

[161] I am indebted in this overview to Mary Clark's first chapter in her small work on Augustine. Mary T. Clark, *Augustine* (London: Geoffrey Chapman, 1994), 1-12.

[162] *Concerning the Nature of the Good: Against the Manicheans*, ch. 1.

good, and made all things, everything good in the world comes from Him. He continues: "God is therefore above every measure of the creature, above every form, above every order, nor is He above by local spaces, but by ineffable and singular potency, from whom is every measure, every form, every order."[163] God therefore exists on a plane that is outside the comprehension of humankind due to His transcendent nature as the Form of all good things, and as the Creator of all things observable by humanity.

Now this separation was not meant to be so. God created the world and humankind in it, that He might have an expression of His goodness in Creation. Humanity was intended by God to be a representation of the highest good, and was created perfect in the image of God. Here a discussion from *Timaeus* is of value as this work was foundational to the philosophical concepts Augustine embraced, first as a non-believer and later as a defender of the faith. The book's namesake embarks upon a discussion of the creation of the world, stating that the world has not always been but rather had an origin and "came to be by the agency of some cause", a notion which dovetails nicely with the Christian view of the act of creation.[164] Further, the world is an image of its creator, who brought all things from a state of disorder into order, and created all things to be good, that is, to be a perfect representation of Himself.[165] God simultaneously gives His creation the ability to choose, to really choose and make rational decisions which result in real determination for the world around them. For Augustine the rational mind with its ability to choose is the highest representation of the mind of God, who created humankind

---

[163] Ibid, ch.3.

[164] Plato, *Timaeus*, trans. Donald J. Zeyl (Indianapolis: Hackett, 2000), 14.

[165] Ibid.

in order that they might best represent His nature.[166] God then gave humanity choice, accepting the end which would result:

> But to the most excellent creatures, that is, to rational spirits, God has offered this, that if they will not they cannot be corrupted; that is, if that should maintain obedience under the Lord their God, so should that adhere to his incorruptible beauty; but if they do not will to maintain obedience, since willingly they are corrupted in sins, unwillingly they shall be corrupted in punishment, since God is such a good that it is well for no one who deserts Him, and among the things made by God the rational nature is great a good, there is no good by which it may be blessed except God.[167]

Thus God designed humanity to be the highest representation of His image in the created world, gave us the ability to choose to love Him and be in right standing with Him, yet accepted the inevitable decision of humankind to choose to desert Him and accept punishment.[168]

For Augustine, the first sin of humanity is pride.[169] John Rist elaborates upon this: "In identifying pride as the source of sin, Augustine is able to carry through another part of his 'project' for the assimilation of traditionally platonic ideas into a Christian framework."[170] This pride exists in the mind,

---

[166] *On Free Will*, ch. 2.

[167] *Concerning the Nature of the Good*, ch. 8.

[168] *City of God*, XII.22.

[169] This is also the sin of the angels, although not the focus of the present work. Ibid, XII, 1.

[170] John Rist, "Augustine of Hippo," in *The Medieval Theologians: An Introduction to Theology in the Medieval Period,* G. R. Evans, ed. (Malden, MA: Blackwell, 2001), 17.

which though created as the representation of the rational *imago dei*, was corrupted by the first man and woman through their attempt to be "like God". All the works of sin which are done in the flesh are not the source of sin but rather its outworking, for Augustine sees humanity's first wrong choice as a direct result of the human person's desire to lift themselves up to be like God, and instead becoming like the devil.[171] Augustine departs here, late in life, from his footing in Platonism, for in *Timaeus*, the body of a man is created good, like its creator, and becomes evil not through its own choice, but through disease of the mind which sets in to the created body. This disease of mindlessness results in a madness by which humankind chooses to do what is excessive, either pleasurably or painfully. Plato feels that humanity is created inherently good, and only becomes bad by disease of the mind and lack of education.[172] Augustine, however, shows that Adam and Eve's choice to exalt themselves in pride and attempt to become like God was not the result of disease, for humanity was created in the perfect image of God. Nor could it be the result of ignorance, for the first persons walked with God and related to him directly. In this way we can deduce that an Augustinian view of the nature of God is such that in the Garden of Eden, God was still transcendent from the world by virtue of having created it and existing before its creation, yet the gap was closer as humankind was able to relate directly to their Creator. God was immanent in direct conversation with human beings. Yet it was Adam's choice to exercise this God-given free will to lift himself up in pride which resulted in a deeper separation

---

[171] *City of God*, XIV, 3.

[172] "And indeed, just about every type of succumbing to pleasure is talked about as something reproachable, as though the bad things are willfully done. But it is not right to reproach people for them, for no one is willfully bad. A man becomes bad, rather, as a result of one or another corrupt condition of his body and an uneducated upbringing. No one who incurs these pernicious conditions would will to have them." *Timaeus*, 83.

of humankind from God. This separation emphasized God's transcendent nature, damaged the rational mind with which humanity was created, and resulted in sin which was passed down to successive generations.

Adam and Eve, as first parents and progenitors of the human race, affected the future of all humankind by their decision. All future humanity were embodied in Adam, the first man. [173] Thus when Adam chose to sin effectually all humankind chose to sin with him, leading Augustine to posit the doctrine of original sin. Here Augustine shows how Adam and Eve introduced sin into the world by choosing not to love God and be united with Him, but rather choosing to walk away from relationship with the Creator. Further in introducing sin, which stemmed from pride and the human ability to choose, the natural result had to be death, for the soul of a man is immortal but God had to maintain His transcendence from the corrupted even in eternity.[174] Thus the body would perish and the soul would be forever distanced from connection with God.[175] The doctrine of original sin, with its consequences in this world and in the next, will be discussed in more detail in succeeding chapters, as it became a pivotal church dogmatic for the medieval period.

---

[173] "For from that man [Adam] all men were to be derived..." *City of God*, XII.27. Further: "And what he himself had become by sin and punishment, such he generated in those whom he begot; that is to say, subject to sin and death." Ibid, XII.3.

[174] Truly for Augustine, the soul of a person was designed to be the conduit between humanity and God. Carol Harrison so accurately states: "Once the soul disobeys God it diminishes itself and becomes part of the temporal it was created to rule." Carol Harrison, *Rethinking Augustine's Early Christianity: An Argument for Continuity* (Oxford: Oxford University Press, 2006), 176.

[175] *City of God*, XIII.2.

Augustine on Immanence

In Augustinian theology humankind was created to be a mirror-image of God, who is the highest Form of the Good. Humanity, in Adam and Eve, chose to depart from this aesthetic and through the sin of pride became incapable of returning to the glory for which they were created. In becoming separated from God's immanent presence in the world, humanity was not relieved of its responsibility to the good, which was to be acted out in this world. In developing the responsibility of the human person, Mary Clark says: "So the basic laws of morality are present to human consciousness." [176] She goes on: "The human person is free to obey or disobey the moral law, but not free from the obligation to obey it."[177] In eternity a person will no longer be separated from God's transcendent nature by sin, if that person chooses to cooperate with grace in this life and to live a moral life in representation of the highest morals with which God created us. The reward for such a life on earth is eternal life with God, who is there reunited, through His own grace, with His restored creation. Augustine further shows us: "It follows, then, dearly beloved, beyond all doubt, that as your good life is nothing else than God's grace, so also the eternal life which is the recompense of a good life is the grace of God."[178]

How is this grace enacted in the world? God chose to reach for humankind out of His transcendence and to evidence Himself in a real and relatable way in the world. While God is everywhere evident in the created world through general revelation, He chose three specific methodologies to further reveal Himself. First is through His words which have been

---

[176] Clark, *Augustine*, 43.

[177] Ibid.

[178] *On Grace and Free Will*, ch. XX.

recorded for us in Scripture. For Augustine, God is Supreme in His wisdom and His wisdom is a part of His unchangeable and transcendent nature. Where humanity has been given a form of wisdom and rationality, God pre-existed with wisdom as a supreme attribute, thereby embodying the highest Form of wisdom. God's wisdom is then imparted in an understandable way in the Scriptures.[179] The Bible is authoritative because it is God's words, it is also revelatory of God's nature in that it is supreme wisdom recorded for posterity. God used human beings to record His revelation of Himself since through the fall humanity's sense of God was fractured and humanity was unable to deduce the higher aspects of God's nature from general revelation. In *City of God* Augustine writes:

> For if we attain the knowledge of present objects by the testimony of our own senses, whether internal or external, then, regarding objects remote from our senses, we need others to bring their testimony, since we cannot know them by our own, and we credit the persons to whom the objects have been or are sensibly present. Accordingly, as in the case of visible objects which we have not seen, we trust those who have, (and likewise with all sensible objects), so in the case of things which are perceived by the mind and spirit, i.e., which are remote from our own interior sense, it behoves [sic] us to trust those who have seen them set in that incorporeal light, or abidingly contemplate them.[180]

---

[179] For an excellent overview of Wisdom in Augustine and an exposition of the Augustinian concept of learning the Scripture, see Etienne Gilson, *The Christian Philosophy of St. Augustine* (New York: Random House, 1960).

[180] *City of God*, XI.3.

This statement draws for the reader a picture of the vision Augustine has of the Holy Scriptures. They are God's very words. They are His condescended self-revelation, to the writers of Scripture, of His transcendent nature and so represent God Himself as He wills Himself to be portrayed to a world of people who no longer possess the sense of being able to tangibly reach to God.[181]

Augustine affords to the Scriptures the highest authority because they are God's self-representation to the world and are His very words recorded by the human authors.[182] In refuting the beliefs of the Manicheans who did not hold to the value of any holy writ, Augustine shows that Christian doctrine is supported and upheld by Scripture, which because it is sourced in God Himself, lends additional value, credence, and manifest truth to Christian beliefs. He shames the Manicheans with their inability to draw support for their beliefs from any outside source other than their own minds, saying: "Destitute as you are of Scripture authority, of the power of miracles, of moral excellence, depart ashamed."[183] The Scriptures, in showing us the nature of God, are intended to draw humanity toward Him through love. Humankind's highest responsibility as God's creation is to return His love and sin as we have discussed above, is an outworking of humanity having pride in self and refusing to love God as we are intended. Augustine believes the undercurrent of the entirety of Scripture is to teach humanity to love God and to love each other; in this way,

---

[181] The reader may recall the terms immanence and revelation, or self-revelation may be used interchangeably.

[182] James Wiles alludes to the saturation of Scripture in Augustine's writings and its import to his understanding in the introduction to his small index on Scriptural citation in Augustine. James W. Wiles, *A Scripture Index to the Works of St. Augustine in English Translation* (Lanham, MA: University Press of America, 1995).

[183] *Reply to Faustus the Manichean*, XII.6

humanity's love for God is simply returning the love He first showed in creating us.

Augustine does not assert that the meaning of Scripture is entirely self-evident. Some aspects of meaning are to be found from an initial reading of the words of Scripture and some to be found only through deeper study and attention paid to the words of God. Kelly points to Augustine's fourfold sense in which Scripture may be understood, with many passages simultaneously holding multiple layers of meaning.[184] The most important role of the reader is to commit the words of Scripture to memory, to read often, and to learn more of Scripture through understanding its original languages. The student of Scripture begins with those passages which plainly outline aspects of faith and life, then moves into those more complex and obscure passages, drawing upon an increased knowledge and understanding of Scripture as a whole. In this way Augustine employs a hermeneutic of moving from the simple to the more complex, relying upon God's revelation of the meaning of Scripture, which may come not only from reading but may also be derived from learning from others who have also received revelation.[185]

Finally when one accepts the Scriptures as true and authoritative, one sees God Himself revealed to the reader. God's will and actions are evidenced in the world; far from being distant from his creation, He is immanent to the world and acts within it. Augustine states:

---

[184] Kelly, *Doctrines*, 75. Also Augustine, *On the Profit of Believing*, 5.

[185] For more on Augustinian hermeneutics see Jaroslav Pelikan, "Canonica regula: The Trinitarian Hermeneutics of Augustine," in *Collectanea Augustiniana,* Joseph C. Schnaubelt, O.S.A and Frederick Van Fleteren eds. (New York: Peter Lang, 1990).

We cannot listen to those who maintain that the invisible God works no visible miracles.... Therefore God, who made the visible heaven and earth, does not disdain to work visible miracles in heaven or in earth, that He may thereby awaken the soul which is immersed in things visible to worship Himself, the Invisible.[186]

This beautiful portrayal of the actions of a transcendent God reaching immanently into His created world evidences the balance which must be struck, and indeed which is presented in such a balanced way throughout Augustine.

Not only did God reveal Himself through Scripture and in nature, but He also further chose to reveal Himself in the most tangible way through the Incarnation. Augustine tells us: "And though He is everywhere present to the inner eye when it is sound and clear, He condescended to make Himself manifest to the outward eye of those whose inward sight is weak and dim."[187] In Jesus, God's Wisdom and Word took on human form and walked the earth as would any other human being. Chosen for a moment in time, this highest expression of God's immanence represents for Augustine God's determination to reunite fallen humanity to Himself. Although God in His triune nature was already immanent to the world, He chose to send the Son as a physical manifestation of the Godhead into the world, in order to restore fallen and fractured humanity. In this vein Augustine questions the reader: "Why then did He come, seeing that He was already here, except it pleased God

---

[186] *City of God*, X. 12.

[187] *On Christian Doctrine*, I.12.

through the foolishness of preaching to save them that believe?"[188]

If restoration of the purpose of humankind was the intention, in what manner was the operation? Augustine goes to pains to demonstrate the Divine nature was in no way reduced, damaged, or lost when God was incarnated in Jesus Christ. "We need a Mediator," he states, "who, being united to us here by the mortality of His body, should at the same time be able to afford us truly divine help in cleansing and liberating us by means of the immortal righteousness of His spirit, whereby He remained heavenly even while here upon earth."[189] God could not have accomplished the restoration of the created order to its intended purpose without maintaining the dual and co-equal nature of Christ as a man and as God. His divinity was not affected by the mortality of his human body, and his humanity was not corrupted by original sin. Against the Docetists, Augustine argued that Christ had a real and corporeal human body, not merely the appearance of such. Simultaneously against the Arians and others he was positioned to argue in support of Christ's full divinity, thereby establishing orthodoxy which would continue to be refined in succeeding councils, particularly Chalcedon in 451 A.D.[190] As for original sin, God purified the soul of the Son, and although original sin passed down from Adam into Christ's human body, His soul was not affected by original sin. Christ was born "perfectly free from sin either actual or transmitted."[191]

This becomes a difficulty in interpreting Augustinian theology and continues to be a thorn in the flesh of those who read the medieval theologians, where it would seem that

---

[188] Ibid.
[189] *City of God*, IX.17.
[190] For more on this see Clark, *Augustine*, 60ff.
[191] Letter CLXIV, 19.

in order to defend God's impassibility, Christ's ability to sin is weakened. If Jesus was unable to sin due to his divinely created soul and lack of original sin, was He truly human? Augustine states somewhat disingenuously that Christ's body was "like unto sinful flesh in all points, sin excepted."[192] This does little to clear the muddy waters and so this aspect of Augustinian theology must be unpacked. Augustine ascribes to Jesus Christ the ability to freely choose, yet be unaffected by the tarnished nature of humanity which wills the body to choose evil. Indeed, he indicates that even fallen humanity may attain a state of inability to sin with enough of an infusion of the grace of God, as Gareth Matthews shows.[193] In this way, the Son's incarnation is a restoring of God's fallen creation to Himself, a restoration of the perfect created and intended order by which humanity is united with the Father in a perfect god-like state and by desire through love.[194] Augustine also uses the language of medicine, showing Christ as physician, offering the healing which is required to return fallen humanity to its previous healthy state. This medicine is Wisdom incarnate which restores the reason of humankind, freeing it from its sin of pride through the humility of the one who gave up His place in heaven and descended to Earth to be born of a woman.[195] This is an act of God's grace and forgiveness which enables humanity to

---

[192] Ibid.

[193] Gareth B. Matthews, *Augustine* (Malden, MA: Blackwell, 2005). His excellent chapters on Free Will, theodicy, and the problem with evil show that Augustine ascribes the inability to sin both to Christ in His humanity and to the potential within humankind when activated grace allows them to be freed from original sin. Augustine does not unspool his own arguments along this line near as much as the modern reader would prefer, but we will see where our subsequent medieval theologians build upon Augustine's arguments.

[194] For a well-rounded discussion of Christ returning fallen humanity to its intended god-like perfection, a term which he refers to as *recapitulative deification*, and which space here does not permit more than an overview, see David Vincent Meconi, *The One Christ: St. Augustine's Theology of Deification* (Washington, D.C.: Catholic University of America Press, 2013), ch.3.

[195] *On Christian Doctrine*, I.14.

return to its intended state. Augustine demonstrates this in asking: "What could He [Christ], who was willing to lay Himself down as the way by which we should return, do that would be still gracious and more merciful, except to forgive us all our sins, and by being crucified for us to remove the stern decree that barred the door against our return?"[196]

Just as the Son is one with the Father, united in nature and essence, so the Spirit is a co-equal member of the triune Godhead. Augustine takes great pains to explain how this is so in his treatise *On the Trinity*, stating: "The Father , the Son, and the Holy Spirit intimate a divine unity of one and the same substance in an indivisible equality; and therefore that they are not three Gods, but one God."[197] While the modern reader might question such a definitive statement, though the medieval writers would take this concept for granted, we must recall that Augustine lived during the time of the early councils which sought to establish doctrine for the church. Simultaneously, he does not infer that this is an easy concept to grasp noting: "It is difficult to contemplate and fully know the substance of God", a notable understatement.[198]

Augustine labors to overcome the barriers encountered by the fallen reason in thinking about the triune nature of God, and in so doing establishes for future generations a starting point for such discussion. For our purpose here of discussing the self-revelation of God in the person of the Holy Spirit we may gloss over much of the philosophical language with which Augustine works to advocate his position on the nature of God. However we may gainfully glance at the ways in which Augustine describes the Spirit as an immanent

---

[196] *City of God*, I.16.
[197] *On the Trinity*, I.4.7.
[198] Ibid, I.1.3.

presence of God to the world. The purpose of this self-revelation of God is, as Ayres describes it: "the Spirit's mission as the immediate transforming presence of God."[199]

Understanding the role or "mission" of the Holy Spirit is to clearly see the immanent aspect of the triune God in the life of the believer. The believer is called to love God, to accept His grace, and to receive forgiveness of sins and transformation of mind. The Holy Spirit is God's Love which is given to the believer, not as a part of God or an aspect of Him, but as God Himself represented in the life of the believer. Whereas in the Scriptures on a number of occasions the Holy Spirit takes a visible and bodily form, in these days the Holy Spirit is invisible and speaks the love of God into the heart and mind of the believer, thereby allowing union and restoration to humankind. Augustine shows the threefold mission or work of the spirit to be in this manner: belief in God is gifted by the Holy Spirit, grace fills the human heart by the work of the Spirit, and a person's will is subjected to the things of God by the power of this third person of the Trinity.

In stating: "All nations...should believe in Christ through the gift of the Holy Spirit," Augustine points to the purpose of the third member of the Trinity.[200] Augustine explores the Holy Spirit as the gift itself which works within humankind, a gift which is given by God or more specifically by Jesus Christ with his death upon the cross. In 27 instances of the use of the phrase "gift of the Holy Spirit", Augustine exclusively intends to mean the Holy Spirit *is* the gift, and speaks to that concept directly and indirectly. In his exposition of the Psalms, Augustine tells us: "[Jesus] is surely able upon thirsty faith to pour the gift of the Holy Spirit", indirectly

---

[199] Lewis Ayers, *Augustine and the Trinity* (Cambridge: Cambridge University Press, 2010), 228.

[200] *On the Trinity*, IV.20.29.

referencing the Holy Spirt as the gift.[201] Additionally in *On the Holy Trinity*, he devotes an entire chapter to outlining the fact of the gift being the person of the Holy Spirit himself.[202] Further, the Holy Spirit is gifted to us to make the immanent God recognizable to humanity, allowing us to see Him, though He is invisible Spirit.[203] The Holy Spirit is also the love of God in our hearts which empowers us to reach out to God and accept His grace and forgiveness. Thus we see that for Augustine the work of the Spirit is to gift love into the heart of the believer, effecting grace for belief.[204]

Chapter Summary

We have seen in this chapter how Augustine brings to the forefront an emphasis on God's co-equal aspects of transcendence and immanence. Augustine establishes orthodoxy for his generation, for future generations, and for the church, through a careful and balanced focus on these attributes of God. When he speaks of God it is at one moment to draw the eyes of the believer upward and outward from him or herself, looking to God as the Creator. Using *City of God* as a single point of excursus we can review in one passage the balanced manner in which Augustine demonstrates these attributes of God.[205] Augustine shows

---

[201] Exposition of Psalm LXXVII.11.

[202] *On the Holy Trinity*, XV.19.33.

[203] *Harmony of the Gospels*, IV.X.16.

[204] For Meconi, the gift of the Holy Spirit is an indispensable means to achieving deification. Meconi shows that becoming "god-like" is a key facet of Augustinian theology. Here he does not intend the reader to understand that humankind might be lifted up as gods themselves, for that would be to invoke Augustine's foundational problem for humanity which is the sin of pride. Rather deification or becoming "god-like" means that the role of fallen humanity is to be restored to a condition of being like God Himself, in ethics, in belief, in love, and in relationship. Only when humankind's sinfulness is washed away through redemption can we be restored to our rightful place in relation to God. Meconi, *The One Christ*, ch.4.

[205] Particularly Book V.

that God is the supreme Creator and He, not fate, is in control of the events of the world. At the same time, His omnipotence and all-knowing do not trump the responsibility of each person for the choices made in their own free will. In disputing Platonists, he shows how worship of any other god cannot confer true happiness, which is only found in redemption of the fallen human spirit and return to a Godly state.[206] He speaks of a God who no longer requires sacrifice because the ultimate sacrifice has already been poured out, that of Jesus Himself.[207]

Additionally he approaches the fact that no one can even know anything about God except that He has revealed Himself, in part, to a fallen creation.[208] For Augustine, God speaks of Himself through the created order, which reveals an aspect of His nature. More so though, God speaks clearly through the truth which is revealed about God in the person of His Son. This second member of the Godhead took humanity upon Himself in order to show the transcendent God in a corporeal and tangibly immanent way. God in becoming a man provided a way back to Himself, a way which allows the believer to be restored to righteous relationship with the Creator and so to live in a manner glorifying to Him in this world. Additionally, this witness is given in the Scriptures which also are themselves a self-revelation of God and are authoritative for the life of the believer because they were composed by the Holy Spirit Himself through human authors. A fallen yet rational mind cannot comprehend those things we cannot see unless one who has been witness to those things records them for our knowledge. This is the message of the Scriptures for

---

[206] On original sin see particularly Book XIV. For the eternal happiness of the Saints see Book XXII.

[207] Book X.

[208] Book XI.

Augustine, who sees in their words God's revelation of Himself in perpetuity for humankind

We conclude with a passage which in many ways sums up the above discussion and which, all in one statement, shows the variegated aspects of God's nature, humankind's fallen nature, and their need for a Savior. More importantly for our current discourse it speaks to a God who is both outside the ability of humanity to grasp, yet is a God who in His mercy brings humanity back to restoration. He does this by His own self-revelation in God the Son, Jesus Christ the Word of God, and in the presence and person of the Holy Spirit who is gifted to humankind to allow us to know God, to love Him, to accept His grace, and thereby be restored to our Godly state. He states:

> Therefore God Supreme and true, with His Word and Holy Spirit (which three are one), one God omnipotent, creator and maker of every soul and of every body; by whose gift all are happy who are happy through verity and not through vanity; who made man a rational animal consisting of soul and body, who, when he sinned, neither permitted him to go unpunished, nor left him without mercy...from whom is everything which has an existence in nature,,,who also to the irrational soul has given memory, sense, appetite, but to the rational soul, in addition to these, has given intelligence and will...--that God can never be believed to have left the kingdoms of men, their dominations and servitudes, outside the laws of His providence.[209]

---

[209] *City of God*, V.11.

Thus we see Augustine's theology, a theology which not only became orthodoxy for future generations but in and of itself became the fulcrum about which medieval theology would turn, as we shall see in greater detail in the succeeding chapters.

CHAPTER THREE:
TRANSCENDENCE

Anselm and Philosophy of Transcendence

Anselm of Canterbury introduces one of his greatest works with these words: "Of all the things that exist, there is one nature that is supreme. It alone is self-sufficient in its eternal happiness, yet through its all-powerful goodness it creates and gives to all other things their very existence and their goodness."[210] In beginning our discussion of transcendence with these opening words of the first chapter of the *Monologion,* several observations should be made from the outset. First is the particularly Platonist way in which Anselm references God, clearly drawing from an Augustinian influence. God is the one supreme nature, the Form of all things, and establishes all other things by His own existence and power.[211] Anselm uses direct reference to God only as an

---

[210] Anselm, *Mono*, ch. 1. All quotations from Anselm's major works in the next four chapters will be from Brian Davies and G. R. Evans, eds., *Anselm of Canterbury: The Major Works* (Oxford: Oxford University Press, 1998). Quotations from his letters and meditations will be from M.R., trans. *St. Anselm of Canterbury: Book of Meditations and Prayers*, (London: Burns and Gates, 1872). Republished as *St. Anselm of Canterbury: Book of Meditations and Prayers*, Translated from the Latin by M.R. with a Preface by Henry Edward Cardinal Manning, Paul A Boer, Sr., ed. (Veritas Splendor Publications, 2013).

[211] Some question exists as to the extent to which Anselm was familiar with *Timaeus*, the key work of Plato which was utilized by Augustine. It seems most likely that Plato as a whole was not well known in Anselm's time for much knowledge had been lost in the intervening centuries between Augustine and Anselm. Hogg states: "There is even uncertainty whether or not Anselm knew the *Timaeus*. The most solid proposition which can be made in favor of Platonic influence, therefore, is that Anselm derived his Platonism from

aside in these first chapters and explicitly in this work only once, naming the supreme nature simply that or sometime supreme essence or Creator. This is to establish a purely philosophical and logical chain of argumentation by which he proposes to convince his readers of the necessity of the existence of this highest essence. In chapter 28 of the *Monologion* finally some religious language begins to creep in as Anselm connects the supreme essence with spirit, who exists in immutable eternity and without qualification. Chapter 30 introduces the concept of the verbalization of the supreme essence as word, and immediately Word becomes a proper noun. Word is the creative power of the spirit, which is supreme essence, yet the Word shares that same essence and existed co-eternally with the supreme spirit. In chapter 40 the reader should be struck by another change in verbiage as the supreme spirit becomes very personal and is represented as parent to the Word who is child. They are then referenced as Father and Son and the spiritual connection to the philosophical argument becomes even stronger. The Father and Son love each other and the love relationship which they share is both the essence of the supreme spirit and is the third person of this supreme nature. These names however are merely a human construct to attempt to explain the supreme essence. Just as Augustine pointed out through his argumentation that language is merely a sign which points to the thing which exists yet cannot be the actual

---

Augustine." David Hogg, *Anselm of Canterbury: The Beauty of Theology* (Burlington, VT: Ashgate, 2004), 80. However, Gareth Matthews draws a more direct connection between Anselm and *Timaeus* in the *Monologion*, and indicates a further distinction between an Anselmian platonist view of God as the Highest Good versus Anselm's decidedly non-platonist view of God as the Creator *ex nihilo*. Gareth Matthews, "Anselm, Augustine, and Platonism," in *The Cambridge Companion to Anselm,* Brian Davies and Brian Leftow, eds. (Cambridge: Cambridge University Press, 2004), 79. Further, Giles Gaspar considers it most likely that a copy of *Timaeus* existed in the library of Bec during the time Anselm was there, based upon his study of monastic library holdings of the time. Giles E. M. Gaspar, *Anselm of Canterbury and his Theological Inheritance* (Burlington, VT: Ashgate, 2004), Appendix 2.

thing, so Anselm here indicates the names he uses for the supreme essence cannot be the supreme essence in themselves, but "merely gesture towards it rather than pinpoint it."[212] In concluding the *Monologion*, Anselm finally draws the conclusion from his long line of argumentation that the reader has been anticipating form the beginning. "The supreme essence rules and regulates all things. It alone is God."[213] God therefore is supreme essence, supreme nature, Creator, Father, Son, Spirit, love, and the ultimate maintainer of all things in creation. His transcendence is manifest with Anselm, from beginning with philosophy to concluding with theology.

A second observation which we have already begun to draw out from the *Monologion*, is its Augustinian nature.[214] Just as McGrath referenced all medieval theology as inherently Augustinian, likewise Southern, the eminent biographer, notes that in addition to the Bible, "the other all-pervading influence on Anselm's thought...was Augustine."[215] Southern goes on to indicate the very way in which Anselm

---

[212] *Mono*, ch. 65. See discussion by Sandra Visser and Thomas Williams, *Anselm* (Oxford: Oxford University Press, 2009), 117. Augustine, *On Christian Doctrine*, II.3.4-II.6.8

[213] Ibid, Ch. 80.

[214] Davies and Evans in their introduction to *The Major Works* state: "What he says [in the *Monologion*] owes a great deal to his reading of *De Trinitate* (On the Trinity) of St Augustine of Hippo....[Anselm's] main interest, like Augustine's, was in the relationship of the persons [of the Trinity] to one another....[Anselm's] approach is to use pure reasoning, so as to show the rationality of the faith he is seeking to heighten in his readers", x-xi. Southern indicates Anselm's use of language is very Augustinian as well, although that influence seems to fade as he grows older. Southern shows that Anselm's early work and particularly the language of the *Monologion* and *Proslogion* demonstrate structure highly influenced by Augustine, whereas in his later works his Latin becomes more his own, highly stylistic and precise. Southern refers to Anselm as one of the most elegant Latinists of the Middle Ages. Richard Southern, *Saint Anselm: A Portrait in a Landscape* (Cambridge: Cambridge University Press, 1990), 73.

[215] Ibid, 71.

thought about God may be attributed directly to how Augustine wrote. While their language differed somewhat due to the natural evolution of Latin over the intervening six centuries, Augustine and Anselm got to God in the same ways:

> Meditation for Augustine, and for Anselm following in his footsteps, is the mental activity which forms a bridge between knowledge of earthly objects and knowledge of the being and attributes of God. The programme of ascent to God through a succession of mental activities, from images to cogitation, from cogitation to meditation, from meditation to contemplation, is Augustine's.[216]

Thus to read Anselm is to begin with Augustine and then to appreciate how Anselm goes beyond the words, arguments, and rationality of Augustine into a greatness of his own.[217]

The *Monologion* is the best starting point in the writings of Anselm in which to encounter his understanding of the nature and attributes of God, however that work is expounded upon in his subsequent piece, the *Proslogion*. Shannon argues that the *Proslogion* may be considered an extension of the *Monologion*, to the extent that "in the *Proslogion* [Anselm] starts from the place at which he had arrived in the *Monologion*, namely, the contemplation or the experience of God."[218] Indeed whereas the name of God does not appear in the *Monologion* until the final page, it is introduced from the first page of the *Proslogion*: "Abandon

---

[216] Ibid, 77-78.

[217] Matthews states: "Anselm belongs to what we may call the Augustinian tradition in Philosophy. Placing him in that tradition should not be allowed, however, to detract from his striking originality." Matthews, "Anselm, Augustine, and Platonism," 63.

[218] William Shannon, *Anselm: The Joy of Faith* (New York: Crossroad, 1999), 87.

yourself for a little to God and rest for a little in Him."[219] As we saw earlier, sin for Anselm is failing to give God what is owed, and this failure results in unhappiness. If the highest role of the created order is to exist in union with God which results in true happiness, sin interrupts that union with separation and death. Anselm cries out: "Alas, unfortunate that I am, one of the miserable children of Eve, separated from God."[220] This statement displays Anselm's heart, but also shows at the same time his understanding of God's transcendent separation from His creation. From that starting point Anselm embarks upon one of the great treatises in the history of the church, chapter two of the *Proslogion*.[221]

The rational mind may conceive of God when the human person realizes that He is that-than-which-nothing-greater-can-be-conceived. Simultaneously, God must truly exist because for something to truly exist is greater than for it to exist only in the imagination, and God is that greatest thing. Additionally, God is so great that He cannot even be thought not to exist. However there is a catch to this rationality and logical necessity. Understanding must be coupled with belief, for although God exists necessarily by His nature of that-than-which-nothing-greater-can-be-conceived, He cannot be under-stood except He illumines the mind through faith. The *Doctor Magnificus* expresses his gratitude for this revelation:

---

[219] Anselm, *Pros*, ch.1

[220] Ibid.

[221] Shannon notes: "It is probably safe to say that, apart from biblical texts, there is no text in the literature of religion that has been more frequently commented upon than chapter 2 of the *Proslogion*." Shannon, *Anselm*, 87. Hogg corroborates this point of view in considering the *Proslogion* "among the most famous of medieval works." Hogg, *Anselm of Canterbury*, 89. Although tempting, it is not my intention here to embark upon an in-depth discussion of the ontological argument (which Visser and Williams call "a curiously unhelpful name"), rather to show from the *Proslogion* Anselm's concept of the transcendent God.

"I give thanks, good Lord, I give thanks to You, since what I believed before through Your free gift I now so understand through Your illumination."[222] This is how the balance is struck for Anselm, for God is the greatest thing that can be conceived, and in His perfections naturally exists on a plane that is beyond the comprehension of humankind, yet in His mercy condescends to be understandable and gives pardon to sinners in order that they may return to the role for which they were created. G. R Evans so excellently points to this juxtaposition:

> Anselm's is a towering God, whose unimaginable height of Being is, in a sense, the very thing that makes us know he is there. He saw no need to try to bring down to human level in his thinking a God beyond human comprehension, or indeed any possibility of it....Anselm clearly saw that Christ is God making Himself approachable, and that entirely 'reachable' Jesus does the necessary work of making a bridge.[223]

Anselm elaborates upon his definition of the nature of God which we have seen so far is that of Creator and maintainer of all things, the highest thing that can be conceived, and who exists by and for only Himself. In *De Concordia*, we further see that God is eternal, immutable, foreknows all things which will happen by man's free choice (a difficult argument which we here do not have space to address), and ultimately that God is just. It is God's eternal nature which is particularly emphasized in this work where Anselm states that because God exists in eternity, He does not exist at any single moment of time. This would, by necessity, limit God to

---

[222] *Pros*, ch. 4.

[223] Evans, *Anselm*, 55. This statement speaks to both themes of transcendence and the immanent God in the person of Christ about which we will have greater discussion below.

acting within the bounds of time, rather than outside those bounds as the Creator of time. Further God is just in that He is the source of all righteousness, but not of unrighteousness which is the result of humanity freely choosing to sin. While the transcendent God has created humankind and given them a rational mind and a free will, and even though He knew beforehand they would choose to fail in their created role of loving God, He allowed sin to enter His created order. God causes people to be, but does not cause them to be evil.[224] Thus God receives the good works which people do as their required acts to Him and is just to punish the evil things people do. It is evil which requires the *rectitudo* by which humanity is returned to their right state with God. It is sin which requires God to reveal Himself, because He otherwise exists outside the realm of comprehension or attainment by a shattered creature.

Transcendence in the language of self-abasement

Thus far we have seen Anselm as the logical and rational philosopher who wished to demonstrate truths about God to the unbeliever and bring the believer to a closer contemplation of God. While we can appreciate the genius of the man for his extrapolation and enlargement upon the work of his predecessor, Augustine, we turn now to the man who yearned to be with God. He desired this union to such an extent that separation from God was torture to his soul. Anselm's *Meditations* exhibit a yearning for his soul to be reunited with God, and the pain of separation which is the result of sin. Anselm's 1st Meditation sets the stage for the further discussion of how his language demonstrates his desire for God, and his language is colorful, heartfelt, and in many ways seems extravagant to the modern reader. However in understanding this language, today's theologian

---

[224] *De Concordia*, 1.7.

is reminded of the suffering, which is inherent to our fallen state, for humankind was created to be with God, yet are unable to reacquire that state for which they were brought to be. Anselm begins with instructions to his own soul, to awaken and put distractions aside. He then reminds his soul to remember the *imago dei* and the purpose of its creation by the transcendent God: "Consider what grandeur and what dignity He bestowed on thee in the very beginning of thy creation, and ponder well what loving and what adoring worship thou shouldst therefore pay Him."[225] He then reminds his soul that thanksgiving for the amazing gifts the Creator has bestowed is the first required response, saying: "Are, then, these so incalculable benefits of the Creator inducements enough to thee for continual thanksgiving in return, and for *discharging the debt* of an endless love."[226]

Anselm establishes in his prayers and meditations a position of the believer abased before God, and adopts language which emphasizes this distance. God is the One "whose so unapproached Being is being in so transcendent and unique a sense that He alone truly IS..." and humankind is "overburdened by a load of sins" which require the sinner to "reflect with groans and tears over the blessings which by those same ills thou hast miserably lost."[227] This praise of God and remorse for sin becomes, in his very colorful language, the means by which Anselm establishes the

---

[225] 1st Meditation, S:1.

[226] Ibid, S:2. Emphasis mine and a reminder that this debt is not fully payable though it is required and sin for Anselm is the failure to pay one's debt or to return that which is required by one's lord. In a world heavily influenced by a Norman feudal system, Anselm employs a mode which would be understood by his educated readers, establishing a hierarchical structure of the believer before God. Of this, Wise states: "By sinning, humanity has both incurred a debt of feudalistic honor and affronted God by falling short of God's intentions." Joshua Wise, "Satisfying the Debt to God: A Synthetic reading of Anselm and the Responsibility of the Theologian," Paper presented to the American Academy of Religion Mid-Atlantic Region Conference, 2017.

[227] 1st Meditation, S:3 and S:7.

separation of the creation from the Creator, and paints a portrait of the unimaginably distant God. Sweeney refers to this process as taking place in two steps: first elevation of the addressee, where Anselm lifts up prayers to God, Jesus, Mary, or the Saints, and second this is coupled with debasement of himself and of sinners as a whole, thereby expanding upon the great gap which exists between the humanity and the Holy One.[228] She makes the additional observation that "Because God is too lofty for him to speak to directly, he asks the saints to act as his intercessors."[229] This becomes a key point in considering the meditations and prayers and the reader must be cognizant that Anselm is establishing distance between created and divine with an undoubtable emphasis upon the transcendent God. As we will see in succeeding chapters this is never at the expense of the God who is also fully engaged in the world. Rather it sets the stage for the sinner who must lift their eyes across the great chasm that exists between humanity and God, and most importantly calls for the believer to live out works of merit in this life which are required by God the King. In reference to this balance, G.R. Evans indicates a duality of sense in which we see through Anselm both "a God who is unimaginably remote from human understanding, and the knowledge of a God who is a friend."[230]

In his prayers to the saints, Anselm uses language of self-abasement to display to the meditative reader the position of the sinner who cannot attain to the glory of God. In his prayer to St. John the Evangelist, Anselm begins with establishing the lofty position enjoyed by the saint as one who is close to God. He states: "Holy and blessed John, chief

---

[228] Eileen C. Sweeney, *Anselm of Canterbury and the Desire for the Word* (Washington, D.C.: Catholic University of America Press, 2012), 18.

[229] Ibid.

[230] G. R. Evans, *Anselm* (Wilton, CT: Morehouse-Barlow, 1989), 37.

of the evangelists of God, best beloved of the apostles of God....I know, sir, what power you have through that same friendship by which you can do what you wish before God."[231] He then establishes his own position as one who does not deserve to speak to God or even to St. John by virtue of the blackness of his sin:

> But alas for my wretched state, how my sins cry out against me! Sins, sins, the more considered, the more horrible you become!...What does he lose, I say, what hardships does he endure, who is forced away by your malice from the love of God to which he could hold by innocence, to become abhorred of God and all his creatures?

Here and in many cases, Anselm speaks directly to incorporeal recipients of his verse, addressing sin directly as though it were a person, or speaking to his own soul. He calls himself abhorrent and an enemy of God and in his sorrow over his sinful state cries out: "Let my limbs be wrenched apart by torments, let my inside be consumed with dryness, let there be an uproar in my inmost being." He then returns to his fervent petition to St. John pleading: "O you compassionate friend of God, have compassion on one so needy."

His need is for one who is close to God to intercede, that Anselm (and in his passion representing all of fallen humanity) may be restored and not condemned by God. In this manner he entreats: "John, John, if you are that disciple whom Jesus loved, I pray you, by that very thing, let me, by

---

[231] All quotations in this section are from *The Prayers and Meditations of Saint Anselm*, trans. Benedicta Ward (Harmondsworth, UK: Penguin Books, 1973), 157-162 (prayer to St. John) and 141-156 (prayer to St. Paul). Space does not permit the reproduction of the entirety of these prayers, and the reader must be content with select passages which illustrate the style and overall tone of Anselm's language.

your prayers, be that sinner whom Jesus forgives." This is further seen in Anselm's prayer to St. Mary, where he both emphasizes the distance between not only himself and God caused by sin, but between himself and his intercessor, whom he begs to entreat on his behalf to God. He genuflects before the Mother of the Lord, saying: "Good Lady, a huge dullness is between you and, so that I am scarcely aware of the extent of my sickness. I am so filthy and stinking that I am afraid you will turn your merciful face from me. So I look to you to convert me, but I am held back by despair, and even my lips are shut against prayer."[232] Thus not only can the penitent, in Anselm's view, not even reach to God, but cannot reach even to their intercessors and must rely upon the grace of the elevated to hear prayers which can hardly be offered aloud.

This language of distance is echoed throughout the prayers of Anselm and in establishing the transcendence of God we discover in his prayer to St. Paul a new development. Not only is Anselm unable to reach to God and must instead reach to an intercessor who will speak to God on his behalf, in fact he equates sin and separation from God with death in this world. Anselm prays: "St. Paul, I came to you as a sinner to be reconciled, and lo, when I am in your presence, I find that I am a dead man to be raised."[233] And further: "As a wretch I came, and I find I am the most wretched of all. I came to you as one living and accused; and lo, before you I am dead and condemned."[234] Here the language of grief over sin and separation from God is taken to the next level where sin and separation are in fact a form of spiritual death in this world. Eternal death is separation of the creature, who was made for relationship, forever from God. Drawing upon the

---

[232] *Prayer to St. Mary.*

[233] *Prayer to St. Paul.*

[234] Ibid.

narrative of the New Testament where in Acts chapter 20 Paul revives Eutychus who has fallen to his death, Anselm equates himself with the dead man and succors the dynamism of St. Paul to revive him from his dead and sinful state. Anselm also envisions St. Paul as a mother who watches over and cares for the young in the Lord and refers to him often by this moniker. The only way to return from separation is to overcome death, which restitution is in the power of St. Paul to give. Anselm beseeches the saint: "O mother, well known for your love, your son knows the heart of a mother's goodness. Show him to God, you who have brought him back to life and cared for him living. Pray to him for your son, who is his servant; pray to him for his servant, who is your son."[235]

While it may be easy for the reader of Anselm to get lost in this language of self-abasement and fervency of outpourings of the soul, it must be remembered first that the style of the day was excellently employed by Anselm and second he is establishing a baseline from which to reach an understanding about God.[236] Most of these meditations and prayers were written quite early in his life and in fact are preceded by only one major work, the *De Grammatico*. In the meditations and prayers, Anselm emphasizes both God's great distance and the inability of the rational creature to reach or understand Him on its own. Only that rationality which is made in God's image coupled with the God who

---

[235] Ibid.

[236] Of this perceived wordiness, Southern writes: "The religious conscience of the time was developing a great partiality for prolonged outpourings. The danger that they would degenerate into meaningless vapourings is only too clear: they often did so. What was needed was someone who could speak this language of self-revelation with power, and add to it a new theological insight. Self-revelation and theological insight were just the qualities which Anselm could contribute." R. W. Southern, *Saint Anselm: A Portrait in a Landscape* (Cambridge: Cambridge University Press, 1990), 99.

condescends builds a scenario in which He allows Himself to be understood in part. Building upon this dichotomous view of God, Anselm later produced the *Monologion* and *Proslogion* which both speak to God's existence by necessity and to God's gracious revelation of Himself. Throughout his life, Anselm sees the position of the sinner as so far below the righteous God that help is needed to even reach out to Him. For this reason he pleads with the saints for their intercession.

The God who dwells in unapproachable light

Where Anselm, and Aquinas as we will see later, were true scholastics, men of the books, Bernard is characterized far more so as a man of the spoken word and a man of letters. The bulk of his theology therefore must be gleaned from interactive works which were recorded later and written down for posterity, but which at the moment of their origination were either sermons, homilies, or letters written to specific persons.[237] While Bernard was very conscientious of the enduring nature of these works, and engaged in a lifelong process of collecting and collating his recorded sermons, editing them and providing for a process of improvement, the current reader must be aware that he did not primarily write for a scholastic audience but rather presented for a relational one. Simultaneously his reach during his lifetime cannot be overstated and his influence in

---

[237] G. R. Evans sees Bernard's theology as best understood through two lenses. The first is monastic theology with an emphasis on obedience and observance of the rule of St. Benedict, as interpreted and applied by the Cistercians. The second is academic theology where she sees his contribution as primarily where he offers a Christian philosophy with its emphasis upon loving God coupled with an intellectual spirituality. This last is drawn primarily from his discussions in Book V of *On Consideration*, which we will explore in depth below. G. R. Evans, *Bernard of Clairvaux* (Oxford: Oxford University Press, 2000), chs. 2&3.

the Roman Church of Western Europe was profound. Daniel-Rops writes: "Called upon by the conscience of Christianity to intervene in the affairs of the world, conscripted to arbitrate political quarrels simply because he was considered a true spokesman of God, the great white monk was constantly obliged to leave his dear monastery of Clairvaux and travel the highways and byways of the world."[238] Although a humble Cistercian monk, he was uniquely positioned in both his place in history and his personal ability to speak to kings, correct even the pope himself, establish doctrine and major movements of the church in his day, and in all ways to exert his influence in the spheres of religion, politics, war, and peace.

Bernard is certainly familiar with Augustine, although he approaches the learned father differently than did Anselm. Bernard shows his familiarity with Augustinian theology most clearly in his *Treatise on Grace and Free Will*. Mabillon states in his introduction to the Life and Works of Saint Bernard: "But how greatly he profited from the reading of the Fathers, especially from S. Augustine, is easily shown by his *Treatise de Gratia et Libero Abitrio*, which is a kind of learned and able summary of Augustine's teaching on that subject."[239] Like many of the writers of his day to include

---

[238] Henri Daniel-Rops, *Bernard of Clairvaux* (New York: Hawthorne Books, 1964), 87. The term "great white monk" refers to the fact that Cistercians wore white as opposed to the black of Benedictines. Daniel-Rops' work is unapologetically sympathetic to Bernard, although the saint is by no means an easy character to accept. He is often heavy handed, high-brow, condescending, and his humility strikes of false humility. Even Thomas Merton in the forward to the same work notes that some may love the man and some may dislike him. There are few readers for whom a middle ground presents itself. Merton avers: "Nothing remains to be said except whether the reader may like St. Bernard or not, whether he may understand St. Bernard or not, he can hardly fail to recognize that he is face to face with an imposingly important personality." Ibid, 7.

[239] John Mabillon, General Preface to his "Second Edition of the Works of S. Bernard," in *Saint Bernard of Clairvaux: Collection*, multiple translators (Aeterna Press, 2016. Kindle edition), S:XXV.

Anselm, Bernard does not often invoke the name of Augustine nor directly attribute his concepts to his predecessor, yet the undercurrent of Augustinian theology is felt throughout his writings. In addition to the *Treatise on Grace and Free Will*, which we will explore below in depth, Bernard's use of Scripture reflects that of Augustine. The extent to which Bernard was steeped in Scripture will become clear and his continuous reference to the words of the Bible throughout his teachings makes it difficult for the reader to understand where Scripture leaves off and Bernard begins. The Reverend Hedley in his introduction to Bernard's sermons for Advent and Christmas states: "St. Bernard knew St. Augustine well, and he had learnt this fashion of using Holy Scripture from him. St. Bernard's mind and heart were steeped in the Scriptures, and it comes natural to one to whom the text is so living and real to treat it as holding a lesson in every word and syllable."[240] This emphasis from Bernard is the particular flow of Augustine into the 12th century.

That Bernard saw God as transcendent from His creation, great in majesty and splendor, and distant from humanity, is evident. The words of the Groom to His Bride in the *Commentary on the Song of Songs* speak clearly to this separation:

> But to be drawn up through the clouds, to penetrate to where light is total, to plunge through the seas of splendor and make your home where light is unapproachable, that is beyond the scope of an earthly life or an earthly body. That is reserved for you at the end of all things, when I shall take you, all glorious, to myself, without spot or wrinkle or

---

[240] J. C. Hedley, Introduction to "Sermons of Saint Bernard on Advent and Christmas," in *Saint Bernard of Clairvaux: Collection*, multiple translators (Aeterna Press, 2016. Kindle edition).

any such thing. Do you not know that as long as you live in the body you are exiled from the light?"[241]

This is an example of the stylistic language employed by Bernard in his *Commentary on the Song of Songs*, one of his most revered works. Again the reader must remember that these were spoken words initially, although later collated and edited somewhat for posterity. This image of God's perfection as light that is so bright the human frame is denied approaching it will be woven throughout the Commentary particularly. It speaks of the separation of God from humanity, a separation which cannot be remediated except that God takes action Himself. Bernard goes further in this passage to say, again in the words of the Groom: "The time will come when *I shall reveal myself*, and your beauty will be complete just as my beauty is complete, *you will be so like me that you will see me as I am*."[242] This then is the only way humankind can be restored to a place of perfection such that they can fulfill their intended purpose of relationship with the Creator in perfect love. God must reach down from His transcendent state and enact for humanity this restoration of their intended condition and state.

Human beings are certainly unable to overcome sin on their own. Only God is able to reach into the world and provide a means of salvation, a means which is enacted by grace. Human beings work together with grace in reaching out to God, and the will consents to receive grace, and further to continue to live out a life which finds favor with God. In *On Grace and Free Will* Bernard brings us this excellent passage:

> [God] joins us to Himself through consent; and, by supplying to our consent the opportunity of

---

[241] *Commentary on the Song of Songs*, Sermon 38: Ignorance of God leads to Despair; the Beauty of the Bride, S: 5.

[242] Ibid. Emphases mine.

performance, by means of our manifest work He that works in us makes Himself known outwardly....The beginning of our salvation is, therefore, without doubt from God; neither is it at all by our means, nor is it with our help. But the consent of the will and the work performed, although they do not originate from us, nevertheless are not without us.[243]

This then can be the only way the gap between the transcendent God and fallen humanity can be bridged, the only way sin may be overcome. For when God provides a means of salvation, and the Holy Spirit enacts love in the human frame, the human being must still cooperate with that grace and love to consent that it be enacted in their lives.[244]

In considering sin and its enduring effect upon humankind, Bernard approached the subject somewhat differently than did Anselm. Anselm, who desired to differentiate his position from the commonly held view at the time, did not see the serpent or the Devil as an active participant beyond the act of original sin. That is, Anselm wished to ensure that the act of propitiation was not one of paying the Devil a ransom for the goods (humanity) which he held by right. Rather we have

---

[243] *On Grace and Free Will,* Ch. XIV. Tamburello adds in his excellent commentary on this passage: "Ultimately, everything depends on grace, and grace is the context in which even our response is enacted. While God does what is proper to God, however, we must do what is proper to us. God can no more do the consenting for us than we can do the motivating and the guiding for God." Daniel E. Tamburello, *Bernard of Clairvaux: Essential Writings* (New York: Crossroad, 2000), 55.

[244] Bernard tells us: "For we are not able to exist here in this world entirely without sin, or without misery; although we are able, by the aid of grace, to avoid being overcome by sin, or by misery." *On Grace and Free Will,* VII. Grace flows from the presence of God the Holy Spirit in the life of the believer, and enacts love which is returned to the Father, thereby reinstating the role of the created in communion with the Creator.

seen that Anselm sees the Atonement as an act of the God-man repaying the debt that is owed by humanity to God, an act necessitated by God's very nature and perfection. Bernard seemingly comes full circle in defending the rights of the Devil, in the context of God permitting the Devil's continued ownership over humanity. Particularly in his argumentation against Abelard, Bernard emphasizes the enormous nature of the Incarnation and Atonement, and the humility of humankind which must be the result of it.[245] It is only through the Atonement that grace is enacted to allow humankind to love God in the way they were intended. Even so, the believer must cooperate with grace through consent as we have seen above. Evans in her excellent discussion of Bernard's view of sin notes:

> Where Anselm thought in terms of God's having raised the humanity in Christ to one with his divinity, Bernard was speaking for his own contemporaries in talking of the 'descent' and humiliation involved [in the Incarnation]. He insists that so startling an act, so extreme a departure from immutability into mutability as God's becoming man, could only be accounted for by a compelling necessity.[246]

For Anselm that necessity was what God was owed to His own perfection in returning a disgraced creature to the status for which it was made. For Bernard that necessity is the love the creature owes back to its Creator and which in

---

[245] In the current work we will not dwell upon the nature of the conflict between Bernard and Peter Abelard. It is one of those messy and controversial issues of Bernard's day, and in considering the person himself it cannot be swept aside. However for the present discussion it bears little weight.

[246] Evans, *Bernard*, 85.

the end results in the state of bliss for which the creature was made.[247]

In *On Consideration* we find Bernard's most theologically concise work as he elaborates his positon on God's transcendent nature. "God is eternity, God is love. He is length without extension, breadth without distension. In both cases He exceeds the narrow limits of space and time....The Godhead stands firmly fixed, immovably self-consistent. Consider 'height' as corresponding to the Divine power, 'depth' to the Divine wisdom."[248] This letter written to a former pupil, who at the time of the letter had become Pope Eugenius, is personal, philosophical, and theological all in one volume. Bernard begins with care for the health of the Pope and a reminder for the Pope to remain humble. Bernard embarks upon an adjuration for the Pope to remember the purpose of the holy office is to care for the people of the church and uphold the Apostolic decrees. He then speaks to some specific activities which were occurring within the walls of the Lateran where members of the Pope's council were involved with taking bribes and paints a picture of the ideal Pope and what his activities should be. Finally in the fifth and final book of this great letter, Bernard launches into one of his most carefully crafted theological works, written for that purpose and for a man who understood theology, and therefore not prepared in the stylistic language of homily.

Departing from his instructions for the Pope, in Book V Bernard encourages Eugenius to the contemplative lifestyle, where consideration of the things of God leads the penitent to God Himself.[249] For Bernard, the contemplative life

---

[248] *On Consideration*, Book V, Ch. XIII, S: 29.

[249] Of the instructions to the Pope and the direction these take through the book, Ratisbonne declares: "Thus, in the instructions addressed to Eugenius, and having determined the Pontiff's relations with the things of this world, he

requires one to rise above and beyond his senses, to embrace the Holy Spirit who guides one into all things of God.[250] The person who seeks God cannot distance themselves entirely from this world, for we are called to bring others to a knowledge of the greatness and goodness of God. However, Bernard develops the lifestyle of the one who considers or meditates upon God as existing in three senses. The first is economical, where the believer "makes systematic use of the senses and of sensible things in daily life so as to win the favour of God."[251] The second sense is estimative in that the believer "wisely and diligently searches everything, and weighs everything, to find God."[252] Finally the third sense is speculative, and the contemplation of the believer "retires within itself, and so far as Divine help is given, detaches itself from human affairs in order to contemplate God."[253]

God exists by His very nature in a realm outside of human understanding. To even contemplate God requires faith, then faith is balanced in humanity by the reason which God created in us. Faith and reason combined do not equal to full understanding, for as we have seen God exists in

---

transports him into the invisible world, into the sphere of divine ideals, and initiates him into the science which is acquired, not by the activity of the mind, but by the contemplation of a purified intelligence." Abbe Theodore Ratisbonne, *St. Bernard of Clairvaux: Oracle of the Twelfth Century* (Rockford, Ill: Tan Books and Publishers, 1991), 286.

[250] "So then the things which are above are not taught by words, they are revealed by the Spirit." *On Consideration*, Book V, Ch. III, S: 5. Evans breaks this down somewhat differently: "Three kinds of *consideratio* can be identified in Bernard. The first is practical, employing the evidence of the senses in the endeavor to behave well in the sight of God; the second is scientific, knowledge oriented, that is, attained by diligent study of all the evidence so as to find God; the third is speculative, involving a direct intellectual apperception of the truth, which becomes possible to the soaring spirit when it throws itself upon divine assistance." Evans, *Bernard*, 54.

[251] *On Consideration*, Book V, Ch. II, S: 4.

[252] Ibid.

[253] Ibid.

unapproachable light. Bernard says that if further inquiry is required, then a full understanding of a thing has not been attained. In God, further inquiry is always required by the believer, thus the importance of the life of consideration, contemplation, meditation, and prayer. Faith can exist without full understanding; indeed it is the relationship of faith to inquiry which makes human persons unique among the rest of the creatures. Further on in Book V Bernard shows the reader: "Faith is, by the exercise of the will, a sure foretaste of truth not yet manifested."[254] This simple line draws for the reader a sure understanding of the import of consideration for Bernard, in that he sees the contemplative life as drawing the believer away from things of this world and closer to things of God. By the Holy Spirit a Christian is able to believe fully in that which they cannot see, and simultaneously to embark upon a lifestyle of walking in the world where favor is gained with God through good deeds coupled with a spirit lifestyle which draws the believer closer to God's presence by faith and contemplation.

Here is where a connection may be made in Bernard between the contemplative life of the spirit and the life which is lived and requires adherence to ethics. Where Evans does not consider Bernard to have made great original contributions to the realm of philosophy, Gilson highlights the originality of Bernard in another area, that of mystical theology.[255] For Bernard, humanity's distance from God is primarily caused by failing to fulfill their calling, that of loving God. The apprentice on the road to God begins from a position of fear, fear of God's judgement for sin. This sin is inherent in the human creature, as our animal nature tends toward sin now after the Fall, and leads to death, which was not intended by the Creator from the beginning at all. Fear and sin thus

---

[254] Ibid, Book V, Ch. III, S: 6.
[255] Evans, *Bernard*, 52.

separate God from humankind. However, as the believer moves along the path toward loving God, the Holy Spirit enacts love in him or her, bridging the gap with a transformation of the human person. It is only by this transformation that humanity is able to return to the state of bliss for which they were created and return to God the love by which and for which He created them. Human beings are unable to love fully and perfectly, because of the natural sinful state into which all of humanity is born, although if it were possible this love would constitute repaying the debt to God. While God would always be transcendent from His creation and exist outside of His created realm, humanity's great distance from God is a result of sin, which fractures the *imago dei* and causes humanity to be unable to fully love God.[256]

Bernard establishes God's distance from His creation beginning particularly in Chapter VI of Book V of *On Consideration*. Here we see God exists eternally, an attribute which is shared by no one but the other members of the triune Godhead. God exists for Himself; He derives none of His existence or purpose for existing from the behest of any other thing or person. God holds the existence of all other things outside Himself in His hands; all other things exist because He does. Thus the whole universe is dependent upon God for its creation and remains dependent upon God for its continued sustainment. The *Mellifluous Doctor* writes: "And so, in a certain sense, He is alone, who is the source of His own existence, and of the existence of all beside."[257] God

---

[256] For a full discussion of this see Etienne Gilson, *The Mystical Theology of Saint Bernard* (London: Sheed and Ward, 1955). Almost the entire book is dedicated to the variegation of this concept in Bernard. One quote particularly stands out: "The beatitude of heaven is union with God Who is Charity. Therefore, to restore in the heart of fallen man the life of charity which ought never to have been extinguished in it, is to bring him nearer step by step to the life eternal which is to be." Gilson, *Mystical Theology,* 85.

[257] *On Consideration*, Book V, Ch. VI, S: 12.

does not exist in any material form, rather all matter was brought into existence by His creative act. God exists outside of space-time, by nature of the simple reason that He created it. The Creator cannot live within His creation or dependent upon it in any way. God is mystery and logic, and philosophy can point the way but ultimately will fall short of reaching to God because He created human reason, and by His very nature exists outside of and beyond that reason. Bernard states: "God is incomprehensible; but you have apprehended not a little if you have ascertained this much about Him, that He is nowhere who is not enclosed by space, and the He is everywhere who is not shut out by space."[258] And further, in a spatial sense speaking of the moment of creation: "You must not ask where He was, except Himself there was nothing. Therefore He was in Himself."[259]

God as the Perfection of all things

Thomas Aquinas takes quite a different approach than our previous writers to all the areas of study we have already explored, and this observation will be developed in successive chapters. His viewpoint may be attributed to a variety of reasons, not least among which are his brilliant mind and sense of organization. An additional factor is his interaction with the universities, which simply did not exist in the time of Anselm or of Bernard. He was highly educated in the earliest universities in the world, and was so accomplished he was invited to instruct at the University of Paris, the most prestigious center of learning in all of Europe. These years at Paris, first studying under Albert the Great and then continuing as a teacher, developed Thomas' mind and depth of knowledge in philosophy and theology. His mind and his pen were so sharpened to a point that after his

---

[258] *On Consideration*, Book V, Ch. VI, S: 14.
[259] Ibid.

death when the subject of his canonicity was approached, it was his writings that were considered the miracles which he produced.

We remember from Chapter One the genius of Aquinas may be seen in his synthesis of Platonism and Aristotelian logic. McInerny refers to Thomas' amalgamation of Aristotle with Christian belief to form doctrine as "Thomas' big picture" and the same could be said of Thomas bringing Plato and Aristotle into the same discussion.[260] This theme will repeatedly be addressed throughout the subjects addressed in this work. Ramos notes in several locations the method Thomas employs of bouncing one philosopher against the other. He will interject Augustine and neoplatonist viewpoints only to counter them with Aristotle.[261] Pieper explores this further in stating: "The simple fact is that those who have dubbed Thomas with the epithet 'Aristotelian' have not hit the mark."[262] Rather Thomas "frequently defends Plato against Aristotle; he points out that Aristotle, in his polemics, often did not consider the substance of what Plato said, the *veritas occula [obscured truth]*, but only the superficial phrasing, the *sonus verborum* [mere sounds]."[263] Gilson expands on this to add that Thomas in fact "drew...on anyone he found useful for his work. We must never forget that his only reason for studying Aristotle was to be better

---

[260] Ralph McInerny, *A First Glance at St. Thomas Aquinas* (Notre Dame: University of Notre Dame Press, 1990), 42.

[261] In the introduction to *Dynamic Transcendentals*, Ramos shows in some areas Thomas prefers the neoplatonist approach. She writes: "The intimate connection that exists between exemplary causality and finality shows an Aquinas more indebted to Plato and Neoplatonism that to Aristotle." Alice Ramos, *Dynamic Transcendentals: Truth, Goodness, and Beauty from a Thomistic Perspective* (Washington, D.C: Catholic University of America Press, 2012), 6.

[262] Joseph Pieper, *Guide to Thomas Aquinas, 3rd ed.* (San Francisco: Ignatius Press, 1991), 43.

[263] Ibid. Emphases original.

prepared to carry out a work he intended to be primarily theological."[264]

To begin a conversation on the Thomist approach to theology proper, we must introduce a discussion of essence, person, and substance. Pieper proposes an argument which firmly interlinks the concepts of essence and existence, showing that for Aquinas these starting blocks must be considered together and simultaneously in order to think about God. When we ask, "What is a thing?" we are presupposing its existence and commenting merely upon its essence or substance. Likewise when we ask "Does such a thing exist" we are considering the substance of the thing to describe it and to question its reality. Aquinas shows when it comes to discussion about God, the two go hand in hand. Pieper describes this duality as being "interested in the *essentia*, the 'inwardness,' to be sure, but also in the *existentia*, the 'thereness.'"[265] God is pure essence, that is, His being exists on a higher plane that any substance. God is not composed of matter, is absolutely simple (in the philosophical sense of not being composed of parts), and exists by and for Himself alone.[266] Simultaneously He is a person, not in the flawed imitative manner in which a human being is a person, but

---

[264] Etienne Gilson, *Thomism: The Philosophy of Thomas Aquinas*, trans. Laurence K. Shook and Armand Maurer (Toronto: Pontifical Institute of Medieval Studies, 2002), 7. This may be a bit of an overstatement as by this time Aristotle was already intrinsic to the curriculum at both Naples and Paris.

[265] Pieper, *Guide*, 135. Emphases original.

[266] For an excellent discussion of divine simplicity and its importance to understanding Thomist theology see Christopher Hughes, *On a Complex Theory of a Simple God* (Ithaca, NY: Cornell University Press, 1989). Although commentary on this subject does not feature prevalently in the current work due to space limitations and owing to an emphasis on Aquinas' notion of God's knowability, an understanding of simplicity contributes greatly to our current considerations of God's transcendence. It is due to His simplicity that He exists on a plane completely separated from the created order and is impossible to describe without using the automatically self-limiting medium of human words and phrases.

God is in fact the Form of "Person". In the *Summa Theologiae*, Aquinas informs the reader that "'Person' signifies what is most perfect in all nature---that is, a subsistent individual of a rational nature. Hence, since everything that is perfect must be attributed to God, forasmuch as His essence contains every perfection, this name 'person' is fittingly applied to God."[267] In this manner of speaking, Aquinas describes God in terms of the Forms, drawing a neoplatonist connection back in time both to Augustine and to Anselm.

Aquinas then goes beyond Platonism, as he does in nearly every case, applying the Aristotelian concept of primacy, with its attendant notions of causation and necessity, to an understanding of the nature of God. He first refutes Anselm's ontological argument by stating the unbeliever simply refuses to admit that God is that-than-which-nothing-greater-exists, and applies logic to his five proofs for the existence of God.[268] The first of these is his "argument from motion," where he demonstrates from Aristotle that all things that are moved must have a Mover, an initiator of movement. If this is true, that all things that are moved or changed require a Mover, then one must work back logically to the first Mover that moves all the rest. Davies tells us Aquinas "concludes there must be a first cause of things being changed or moved. For there cannot be an endless series of things changed or moved by other things since if every change in a series of connected changes depends on a prior changer, the whole system of changing things is only derivatively an initiator of change and still requires

---

[267] *ST,* I-I.29.3.
[268] *ST,* I-I.2.3.

something to initiate its change."[269] For Aquinas it is clear this First Mover is God.[270]

In Aquinas, this is a key consideration, that God by His will set all things in motion. Motion for Aquinas and for Aristotle is energy and potency, the force of growth, gravity, and potential which exists in all things.[271] God then is the greatest expression of potency and initiation, setting all things in motion by and for Himself. Just as there cannot be an endless procession of causes so there cannot be an endless series of existence either. God is His own existence and existed in and for Himself before all things. Davies explains: "Given that there are things in whose nature or essence existence is not included, there is something which produces their being, something which makes them to be though nothing makes it to be."[272] God's nature presupposes existence whereas nothing else in the universe exists in and of itself. All things were brought to be where God was not brought to be. He simply is and always was.

Aquinas goes beyond the argument from motion in the early portion of the *Summa Theologiae* to describe the transcendent nature of God as the highest expression of all things. He addresses the simplicity, perfection, goodness, infinity, immutability, eternity, and unity of God, in each chapter demonstrating that God exists as the Form of all

---

[269] Brian Davies, *The Thought of Thomas Aquinas* (Oxford: Clarendon Press, 1992), 28-29.

[270] *ST*, I-I.2.3.

[271] McInerny feels that for Aristotle and for Aquinas by extension, motion is at the very heart of all things. He states: "Since nature is a principle of change or motion, one cannot know what nature is without knowing what motion is." McInerny, *First Glance*, ch. 11. This is his starting point for grasping Thomist philosophy and theology for although motion is act and is the result of potency being put into action, it is still imperfect, in that all things we know decay. Motion stops, life ends, hot regresses to warm. However in God who is the purest potential, all act, all motion, and all potency receive their origination.

[272] Davies, *Thought*, 32.

those concepts. He further exists in such a way that no one could know any of those concepts except they exist in God. Thus God's nature defines not only the existence of all other things, but the fact that anything may be known of Him at all. For Aquinas, God exists on an unknowable level, a plane which cannot be understood by human beings. His infinity of being renders Him incomprehensible and "it is clearly impossible for any created intellect to know God in an infinite degree."[273] Pasnau and Shields iterate this in saying: "Aquinas also believes that certain truths about God's nature are beyond the scope of natural reason" although he appeals to reason in his proofs for the existence of God.[274] What is important in a discussion of God's knowability is that what human beings reason about God comes only from indirect knowledge of him.

At the same time what may be known of God is brought to human understanding by God Himself, who has placed in each person the hope that He exists, and any partial comprehension we may have of the Divine is a response to that hope. Much as Anselm discussed in the *Proslogion*, human beings are created as rational creatures and reason is fittingly applied so that a person may come to a knowledge of God, albeit indirectly. At the same time there exists a two-fold requirement for coming to any knowledge of God and that is reason coupled with belief. Aquinas shows this in the *Summa Contra Gentiles*: "Beneficially therefore did the divine Mercy provide that it should instruct us to hold by faith even those truths that the human reason is able to investigate. In this way, all men would easily be able to have a share in the knowledge of God, and this without uncertainty and

---

[273] *ST*, I-I.12.7

[274] Robert Pasnau and Christopher Shields, *The Philosophy of Thomas Aquinas* (Boulder, CO: Westview Press, 2004), 82.

error."[275] Still, this sharing in knowledge is limited by the incapacity of human beings to attain full knowledge of the divine. Alice Ramos neatly sums up the difficulties of the human mind in comprehending the infinite, and makes a compelling argument, one grounded in Anselmian reasoning. She writes:

> Man's intellect, created as a potency unto the infinite, is meant to reach beyond the data of the senses to the cause and origin of all perceptible things, and also to appeal to this higher source for the knowledge of good and evil. However, once the mind seeks to declare its independence from God, from the origin of all being, truth, and goodness, the human capacity to know the truth is impaired.[276]

Pieper describes this as the moment "our thinking meets the *mysterium* of being."[277] Thus though God is incomprehensible, He is also knowable in part by virtue of His creative act of placing within the human person reason and belief which may be used to find Him.[278]

If God is to be known, even in part, it must be grasped that He exists as the actuality, the Form, and the highest expression of all things. His essence is such that He embodies the perfection of all things. Gilson convincingly states: "The most marvelous of all things a being can do is:

---

[275] *SCG*, 1.4.6.

[276] Ramos, *Dynamic Transcendentals*, 48-49.

[277] Pieper, *Guide*, 137.

[278] O'Meara calls faith a "dark knowing" and shows faith is the "acceptance of the revelation of humanity's 'immediate orientation to God' and its 'special ultimate happiness,'" in both cases citing *ST*, II-II.2.3. Thomas F. O'Meara, *Thomas Aquinas Theologian* (Notre Dame: University of Notre Dame Press, 1997), 88.

to be."[279] In the *Summa Contra Gentiles*, Aquinas shows that God actually exists above and beyond the concept of Forms in that one cannot say, for instance, "Human beings reflect God's image, and are composed of bodies, therefore God must have the ultimate body." By stating that God cannot be composed of both form and matter, and rather exists in a state beyond matter and composition, He is the ultimate being. God transcends matter and composition by His very nature and essence.[280] So in this sense it would actually be limiting to God to consider Him as being the Form of all matter or the Form of body. Rather it is better to consider God's nature and essence as existing on a plane such that matter, and composition are beneath Him. His transcendence beyond anything tangible is ultimate and final.

It further follows that God, as the "prime unmoved mover" and as the highest expression of all things, transcends time and space by virtue of being their Creator. Here we see the argument from motion and the argument from existence culminate in the act of creation. Aquinas presupposes God's creative force in stating: "[M]atter must be produced by God's action since…everything that exists in any way at all has God as the cause of its existence."[281] Pasnau and Shields observe: "In each of his two great *Summae*, Aquinas moves from discussing God's nature to discussing the nature of the created world. All…of the divine attributes…encourage the hypothesis that God is the ultimate source of being."[282] Whereas the world had a moment of initiation, God did not, having existed eternally. Further, God created all things that exist from nothing (creation *ex nihilo*). This is important for

---

[279] Gilson, *Christian Philosophy*, 83.

[280] *SCG*, 1.27.4

[281] *CoT*, 1.69

[282] Pasnau and Shields, *Philosophy*, 121.

if God is the highest expression of all virtues, and He is the perfection of all knowledge, He is also the perfection of all creation, having existed before matter and having brought all matter into existence.[283] Aquinas here distances himself from the Neoplatonism which had heretofore been the foundation of this argument in stating that God did not need to create the forms of things, so that the created things themselves might flow down from the forms of them. Notably, in his Aristotelian way, the *Angelic Doctor* had already demonstrated that while God Himself is the perfection of all virtues in His very nature, simultaneously God's Ideas are themselves the forms of all created things.

Plato referred to Ideas as the forms of things which exist by themselves, outside of matter. However this would imply that a human being can know those things which exist in and of themselves, whereas we know from Augustine this must be reserved solely for God's transcendent mind. Gilson, referencing Augustine's ongoing attempts to rescue anything salvageable from Platonism shows how "Augustine substituted for Plato's Ideas the essences of all creatures united in the divine mind. All things would be created in conformity with these essences, and through them the human soul would know everything" when united with God in eternity. Thus all things that exist are brought into being as mere representations of what exist in their highest expression in the mind of God. Gilson goes on to indicate that for Thomas the divine ideas exist in the mind of God both as exemplars of those things which exist in the created order and simultaneously as the principle by which the created thing can be known. He declares: "We must grant that there exists in the divine intelligence a form in whose

---

[283] *SCG*, 2.16.2. Also *ST*, I.44.4: "[I]t does not belong to the First Agent, Who is agent only, to act for the acquisition of some end; He intends only to communicate His perfection, which is His Goodness."

likeness the world has been created. This we call an idea."[284] The creative act is a natural and necessary outpouring of the divine ideas as the principal cause of all things that we see in the world, to include those non-tangibles such as moral behavior, goodness, and beauty.

A final note must be added to the preceding description of God's creative power. For Aquinas God is omnipotent by virtue of His very nature, substance, and essence. However, to say that God is all powerful, for the Master of Philosophy is not to say that God can create all things. For instance, God cannot create in a manner which is drawn from implicit contradiction. Pasnau and Shields refer to this as God's being unable to bring into being anything from "a class of things that are incompatible with being, things that by their nature are nonbeings."[285] For Aquinas this is less a discussion of God's inabilities as it is a pointed accentuation of God's unwillingness to act outside of the laws of logic which He invented. Further God's omnipotence and God's perfect goodness do not require a perfect creation, although what God put in place initially was free from fault, for He declared it to be good.[286] Humankind was initially created for intimate union with God and, although human beings could never have fully understood God's nature, this relationship was intended to be communal. What went wrong in the Garden is God's creation enacted self-determination, which was a choice God had given them. In doing so, the First People distanced themselves from the state of original grace and communion with the supernatural essence, resulting in

---

[284] Etienne Gilson, *Thomism*, 133.

[285] Pasnau and Shields, *Philosophy*, 126.

[286] Pasnau and Shields note that God's goodness, being perfect in and of itself, does not require anything external to it to be "more perfect." Therefore "God was under no obligation to create a perfect universe, or even a very good universe. God was utterly free to create or not to create, and to create one kind of universe or another." Ibid, 131.

original sin which affected all of subsequent humanity. Dauphinais and Levering describe this effect so well:

> We were created with nature and grace, but original sin damages our nature and destroys our grace. The supernatural life, or grace, leaves the human creature as the result of original sin. In the state of original justice, human beings had been upheld by grace from suffering bodily corruption. After original sin, there is no longer any impediment to the decay of our bodies through aging and disease. The natural life does not leave completely, but rather suffers a terrible wound. The human intellect no longer can see the truth about the world and God clearly. The human will can no longer choose decisively the true good.[287]

This is the greatest separation between God and humanity, for in choosing to exist outside of intimacy with God, the *imago dei* was damaged. All human beings were left in a state such that God's transcendence, which had existed from the beginning, became seemingly irreconcilable to the subsequent human condition.

---

[287] Michael Dauphinais and Matthew Levering. *Knowing the love of Christ: An Introduction to the Theology of Thomas Aquinas* (Notre Dame: University of Notre Dame Press, 2002), 39.

CHAPTER FOUR:
GOD'S SELF-REVELATION IN THE HOLY SCRIPTURES

Medieval Hermeneutics

Just as Augustine was the bedrock of medieval theology so his interpretation of Scripture became the foundation of medieval Biblical hermeneutics.[288] Understanding the way the medieval philosophers read and understood the Holy Scriptures is germane to a discussion here in that all three of the writers we are engaged with in this work were prolific readers of Scripture and in turn utilized the words of scripture at seemingly every juncture. Augustine and the Bible are the cornerstones of theology and philosophy for the Middle Ages and how these two sources are used by the medieval philosophers gives the modern reader an understanding of how they interpreted and applied Scripture. To engage with the words of the Bible as employed by our three thinkers, we must understand in some ways the nature of the medieval hermeneutic.

While the study of hermeneutics would not become an established field until the 19th century, as Gallagher and Damico assert: "Interpretation - the technique of giving meaning to an object by means of clarification and

---

[288] For an overview of medieval hermeneutics and the role of Augustine see the brief but well written introduction to Patrick J. Gallagher and Helen Damico, eds., *Hermeneutics and Medieval Culture* (Albany, NY: State University of New York Press, 1989).

explanation - is an ancient art."[289] Anselm, Bernard, and Aquinas certainly never reference hermeneutics as a study in itself but we can deduce a method from their interpretive application of Scripture, a medieval hermeneutic which begins with Augustine. It must be noted that for Augustine, a hermeneutical structure was already in place, largely established two centuries before him by Origen of Alexandria (c. 185-c. 254). Origen wrote prodigiously, believed in the inspiration of Scripture by the work of the Holy Spirit, and most importantly for our discussion believed that every word of Scripture had a purpose and an intended meaning. Indeed he believed that most of Scripture had a range of meanings, applicable to various audiences and situations of understanding. Nadia Delicata observes accurately that Origen "was the first to apply extensively and systematically the techniques of Hellenistic *grammatica* to the books of the Scriptures." [290] Writing in Greek, he outlined a three-pronged intention of meaning within the Scriptures: first is the literal or obvious sense, second a deeper sense which is detected by the soul of a person educated in philosophy, and third is the deepest, often hidden, spiritual meaning which is revealed by the Holy Spirit. Origen's exegetical method was accepted in his time and elaborated upon by Augustine such that Origen's "method of exegesis reached its culmination in the medieval tradition of the 'four senses of Scripture.'"[291] Augustine's four senses or four primary aspects of engagement with the text are these: polysemy (or the fact that multiple meanings may be derived from the same block of context), the relationship of the parts to the whole (that is, recognizing that context provides meaning, not simply isolated words), the recognition of difference (between words

---

[289] Ibid, 2.

[290] Nadia Delicata, "*Paideia tou Kyriou*: From Origen to Medieval Exegesis" in *Didaskalia* 27 (2016): 37.

[291] Ibid.

themselves in context and comparing sections of a text against itself), and the importance of correcting misinterpretation (erroneous understanding leads to false application).[292] From Augustine the medieval theologians received an emphasis on understanding Scripture to be written allegorically, with the spiritual sense often veiled by this method. This sense of allegory will become evident as we engage with the medieval writers, although in many ways Anselm and Bernard particularly go beyond Augustine in overemphasizing the role of allegory in Scripture. As Thiselton indicates, Augustine offers sober, succinct, historical exegesis which is always accompanied by application.[293] Wood feels: "The restless spirit of Augustine was not fully satisfied with allegory. His developing mind could not ignore the claims of the written word. Allegorical interpretation could be but one stage in the process."[294] Allegory thus became synonymous with the third sense of the meaning of Scripture, common to both Origen and Augustine.

Anselm and Scripture as foundation to philosophy

When it came to the time of Anselm, Augustine's principles of interpretation of Scripture had become normative for students of theology. Anselm proceeded to build upon this base, as he did in all areas of study. While use of Scripture is laced throughout Anselm's work (except for the *Monologion*

---

[292] This discussion is derived in large part from Gallagher and Damico's introduction to *Hermeneutics and Medieval Culture*. They also point out similarities between Augustine's 5th century understanding of the derivation of meaning and that of modern teachers of hermeneutics, such as Paul Ricoeur. As regards erroneous interpretation, we have already seen in Chapter Two that Augustine believed even wrong interpretation, if delivered with the intent of showing the love of God, could still have value.

[293] Anthony Thiselton, *Hermeneutics: An Introduction* (Grand Rapids: Eerdmans, 2009), 115.

[294] Quoted here from Thiselton, *Hermeneutics*, 115.

and *Proslogion* for reasons stated in chapter four), it is most prominently displayed in the *Meditations*. Peppered throughout the *Meditations* are Anselm's frequent references to the words of Scripture, and he calls Scripture as a "witness", evoking imagery of a person testifying on behalf of the veracity of God.[295] He sees the Bible as both the Word of God and the words of God, and the authority to which he grants the words of Scripture is commensurate with their issuance from the very mouth of God. He calls the reader of Scripture to be circumspect considering this authority and to understand the limitations of humanity's imperfect reason, which might by means of fanciful philosophy cloud the understanding.[296] No one can be saved by reading the words of the Bible alone, rather these words are given depth when the reader believes and receives God's gift of grace. The reader is then charged to nurture an understanding of the meaning of the text in order to reach a deeper understanding of God Himself. In this way we can recognize the Bible as God's self-limiting revelation of Himself. Through Anselm we can understand a concept of God's self-revelation from the words of *De Concordia*. Here he calls the reader of the Scriptures to cultivate the seed of the word of God through study of it and reliance upon faith to give deeper meaning.[297] He further indicates that understanding of God is not brought merely by the word but by their meaning, saying: "Obviously mere sound without meaning establishes nothing in the mind."[298] Further an understanding of God is brought not only by reading of Holy writ but in any "perception of uprightness", which through the conscience brings knowledge of God.

---

[295] *First Meditation: Of the Dignity and the Woe of Man's Estate*, S:5.

[296] *On the Incarnation of the Word*, S:1.

[297] *De Concordia*, 2.6.

[298] Ibid.

While the Bible is clearly authoritative as God's words, for Anselm more is needed than merely skimming those words. Scripture is necessary for salvation as it is God's revelation of Himself in a form which is most easily grasped, and understanding of God Himself through the words of Scripture is only enacted by the gift of grace and removal of sin. Additionally it is only when the meaning of Scripture is revealed through the work of the Holy Spirit that knowledge of God Himself becomes attainable. At the same time, God created human persons to be rational creatures, and those creatures will naturally develop concepts on their own which are not explicitly stated in Scripture. In regards to building upon the witness of Scripture Sweeney tells us: "Anselm sees *De Concordia*...as speaking where Scripture is silent, addressing problems that are internal to and implied by the creedal principles of Christianity."[299] Anselm himself states:

> For if at times we assert by a process of reasoning a conclusion which we cannot explicitly cite from the bare wording [of Scripture], still it is by using Scripture that we know in the following way whether the affirmation should be accepted or rejected. If the conclusion is reached by straightforward reasoning and Scripture in no way contradicts it, then (since just as Scripture opposes no truth so too it abets no falsehood) by the very fact that it does not deny what is inferred on the basis of reason, that conclusion is accepted as authorized by Scripture. But if Scripture indubitably opposes our understanding, even though our reasoning appears to us to be impregnable, still it ought not to be believed to

---

[299] Eileen C. Sweeney, *Anselm of Canterbury and the Desire for the Word* (Washington, D.C.: Catholic University of America Press), 12.

be substantiated by any truth at all. It is when Sacred Scripture either clearly affirms or in no wise denies it, that it gives support to the authority of any reasoned conclusion.[300]

The Bible is not merely words about God, it is God's very words. It is these words from the mouth of God which reveal Him to His creation. It is only because human persons have been given rational minds to understand the communication of language the possibility even exists of God being able to discuss Himself in this way. However, owing to God's transcendent nature, He is *ineffabilis*, that is, unable to be spoken about. This concept drives both a discussion of transcendence and immanence in that while God is able to reveal Himself in Scripture, humanity is only able to comprehend a part of God's self-revelation, thereby demonstrating again the distance between God and His creation. Evans points this out quite well:

> The strong impression of God's inaccessibility which pervades Anselm's devotional writings is entirely in keeping with the view that it was, in Anselm's view, in the very nature of language that it should be used to work towards a knowledge of God, but that it is, in the end, impossible to talk about God as he is, because the words themselves...do not permit us to do so.[301]

Thus while Scripture is authoritative as God's very words, it is not a comprehensive manual for life. It must be accompanied by faith and reason in order to resonate the revelation of God into the life of the believer. Vice versa, the

---

[300] Ibid.

[301] G. R. Evans, *Anselm and Talking about God* (Oxford: Oxford University Press, 1978), 35.

rational mind must be subjected to the authority of God's words.

Anselm was a master of the written word and extremely gifted in use of the Latin of his day. His approach to Scripture reflected that attention to detail and he wished to draw from the pages of Scripture and understanding of God Himself. Sweeney feels: "Anselm thinks so deeply about key passages from scripture, he not only transforms them into probing questions, but the notions discussed in these passages become seeds of a philosophical and theological anthropology."[302] Even so, Anselm goes beyond the words of Scripture and particularly in the language of his prayers introduces his own passions as being intertwined with the narrative. His lament is felt so strongly in his Prayer to Christ, where his longing to be free from his own sin colors his use of the words of Scripture. For instance, he introduces the words of Psalm 83:9, "Lord before you is all my desire" then turns those words into an observation that anything good in the soul is from God and it is good to desire to love God, and concludes this section with an entreaty that Christ would grant to his soul the desire to love with abandon. In another passage Anselm quotes the words of the first Gospel in placing himself in narrative. "Would that I might have heard from the angel's mouth, 'Fear not, Jesus who was crucified, whom you are seeking, is not here; he is risen.'[303] He then spins those directs words of Scripture into a deeply personal prayer for Christ's grace as a consolation for not having been there in person. Where Anselm reads the narrative of the cross in Scripture, he reimagines it with a sense of his own suffering for sin, thereby rendering a deeply personal and heartfelt relationship to the characters and

---

[302] Sweeney, *Desire*, 10.

[303] Prayer to Christ, in *The Prayers and Meditations of St. Anselm*, trans. Benedicta Ward (Harmondsworth, UK: Penguin Books, 1973), 96.

events of Scripture. For Anselm the believer must begin with the words of the Bible, but must further internalize the concepts such that in prayer and meditation the words of Scripture form merely the backbone of the language of one in meditation before God. While St. Benedict said little directly about prayer in his rule (assuming that prayer would form the basis of the meditational communities he envisioned), for Anselm "the way into prayer was through meditative reading, with the aim of purity of heart and compunction of tears."[304]

In a liturgical sense, Benedicta Ward adds that the prayers of St. Anselm were so carefully recorded in his day, and were passed on to other individuals and entire meditational communities who used them as a basis for their own communion with God. They became the first of a genre of writing which would be added to the words of Scripture and thereby form the first body of corporate and individual service to God which would grow throughout the Middle Ages to become the liturgy of the Church and of the meditational communities.[305] This in fact extended beyond the cloister, and Ward adds: "The Prayers were available for all, not just the monks. The basis of sorrow for sin applied equally to monks and lay people, self-knowledge was where everyone began."[306] The end result was that while most people of Anselm's day could not read the word of scripture for themselves, they could understand with immediacy the need for their own penitence, supplication for grace, and intimacy with God which would be achieved through meditation.

---

[304] Introduction to *The Prayers and Mediations of St. Anselm*, trans. Benedicta Ward, 45.

[305] William Shannon, *Anselm: The Joy of Faith* (New York: Crossroads, 1999), 57.

[306] Benedicta Ward, *Anselm of Canterbury: His Life and Legacy* (London: SPCK, 2009), 27.

Sweeney in her epic tome makes the observation that Anselm does not employ the most common hermeneutical devices of his time, where many of his contemporaries and particularly his successors embarked upon enormous commentaries on the text of Scripture or engaged in deep discussion of the allegorical meaning of certain passages.[307] While he certainly quotes from the words of the Bible, in most cases it is to underscore a certain point or observation, or to establish the authority with which he speaks on a certain topic. His focus as a philosopher and his desire to build a logical defense of his positions precluded an over-reliance upon the scriptures, and he seems generally content to reference the words of scripture as a side note to his prose

Bernard and medieval allegory

We have alluded above to the extent with which Bernard's thought and writings are saturated with the words of Scripture. Clearly, he was a man for whom the Word was very dear although as we will see he felt comfortable to take a certain amount of license with his application of Scripture.[308] He is certainly aware of the Augustinian four-fold meaning of Scripture and he writes as one to whom revelation of the deeper meaning of Scripture has been gifted. He speaks with confidence and peppers his hearers with the

---

[307] Sweeney, *Desire*, 177. We will explore both of these further in our discussion later in this chapter of Bernard and Aquinas and their respective relationships to scripture.

[308] Today's theologian is most struck by the fact that Bernard takes nearly every verse out of context and seemingly applies the words to whatever he wants them to mean. The important points to remember are first that this was a common medieval stylistic use of Scripture and second that Bernard does not engage in exegesis. He uses the words of the Bible as the foundation of every point of emphasis he is making to the listeners and readers of his day. He feels the words of Scripture are the highest authority to which he can appeal, and as a man of God and leader of the Church, he emphasizes his own authority by invoking the words of Scripture.

words of Scripture, seemingly emphasizing every point with words from the Bible. In his introduction to the *Commentary on the Song of Songs* he alludes to the importance of Scripture in the life of the believer: "And when, as happens, texts of Scripture become bright with meaning for you, then, in gratitude for this nurturing bread of heaven you must charm the ears of God with a voice of exultation and praise, a festal song."[309] Bernard here feels he is enlightening his listeners with truth and revelation from God's word and feels entitled to do so by his position as a man of study and an authority within the Church of his day.

Though the splendor and majesty of God are never far from his mind, Bernard bridges the gap between God and humanity by placing it within the divine will to do so. He tells us: "Such is the way the God whose majesty is so great has *decided to be present* to his creatures: as the being of all things that are, as the life of all things that live."[310] God has determined to reveal Himself in part to His creation in order to restore friendship between Creator and creature and to endow humanity to live with virtue. One way in which He does this is notable in the recorded words of Scripture, which Bernard refers to as the mouth of God. God's very words are spoken in holy writ and as such represent the very voice of God into the world. Though God is distant from us He is also present to us by His miraculous self-revelation. Bernard beautifully points to this act of God bridging the gap: "No one can measure his greatness; no man can see him and live. Yet he who by his very nature is the principle through whom all creatures spring into being, cannot be far from any of us, since without him all are nothing."[311] God has created all

---

[309] *Commentary on the Song of Songs*, Sermon 1: On the Title of the Book, S:9.

[310] *Commentary on the Song of Songs*, Sermon 4: The Kiss of the Lord's Feet, Hands, and Mouth, S:4. Emphasis mine.

[311] Ibid.

things and by His power sustains all things, yet He reveals Himself intimately into the world by His spoken word.

Evans emphasizes the salvific nature of Scripture for Bernard, bringing the reader to a believing knowledge of God. This is true for the individual in "Christian" Europe as well as for the pagan in foreign lands. "Scripture, for Bernard, is the Word of salvation (*verbum salutis*), and for him the Bible was consequently the most important thing he read."[312] Interestingly, while Evans represents Bernard as emphasizing use of the Bible for winning of souls to Christ, Bernard himself in referencing the crusading armies in the Holy Land during his day indicates that preaching salvation to the pagans is not as important as protecting the righteous from harm. In terms of defending the holy cause of war against unbelievers, Bernard writes: "Yet this is not to say that the pagans are to be slaughtered when there is any other way of preventing them from harassing and persecuting the faithful; but only that now it seems better to destroy them than to allow the rod of sinners to continue to be raised over the lot of the righteous."[313] He goes further to state that in the Holy land "there is more need of soldiers to fight than of monks to sing or pray."[314] Bernard's intention is not on the salvation of pagans so much as bringing believers to a right way of life, a lifestyle which finds favor with God and induces love from the creature to the Creator.

With this motivation in mind we must explore the use of allegory by Bernard, for he was one of the most articulate proponents of this style of representing the meaning of Scripture in his day and in the Middle Ages as a whole. Bernard's enormous commentary on the Song of Songs, and

---

[312] G. R. Evans, *Bernard of Clairvaux* (Oxford: Oxford University Press, 2000), 57.

[313] *In Praise of the New Knighthood*, Ch.3.

[314] Letter CCCLIX, *The Community of Clairvaux to the same Celestine* (Pope Celestine as referenced in the preceding letter, CCCLVIII).

its accompanying series of sermons, which in many ways could be considered his life's work, provides the best assessment of Bernard's use of allegory. He only uses the actual word allegory (*allegoria*) two times although he understands the Augustinian nature of the use of allegory in Scripture as derived from the deeper Spiritual sense which goes beyond the obvious, surface, and literal sense of any verse or passage. His first usage of the word *allegoria* is in reference to the story of Elisha asking for favor from his master Elijah, immediately prior to the latter being taken up bodily into heaven. Here Bernard employs the term in the context of this Old Testament passage, using it as an example in our lives today of receiving the Holy Spirit from God. His final use of the term *allegoria* is used in one of his later sermons on the Canticles. Here Bernard outlines his purpose in commenting and preaching from this erotic Hebrew poetry. He states: "My sole concern has been to remove the thick veil of allegory, and to place clearly before you the sense of this secret and delightful intercourse between Christ and His Church."[315] This then is the foundational consideration for Bernard in approaching this section of Scripture, and he even decries his own lack of moral application from these sermons.[316] Rather the point of his preaching on the Canticles was simply to spend time discussing the more mystical elements which are not clearly outlined in these passages, and to bring his readers and listeners to the point of recognizing the relationship of Christ with His Church through these words of Solomon.

The Song of Songs is a love story to be sure, but to Bernard who had embraced his personal role as the bride of Christ and saw the Church as a whole as the Bride of Christ, it can

---

[315] *Sermons on the Canticle of Canticles*, Sermon LXXX: On the Image of God, and the Soul which is made according to the Image; and on the errors of Gilbert de la Porree.

[316] Ibid.

only be a love story evoking the intimate details of that relationship. Also for one who was sworn to celibacy to consider the evocative imagery as anything less pure than the relationship between Christ and Church would be inappropriate. Therefore, Bernard distances himself from the literality of the text, a work which was almost certainly first a love poem, and secondarily a spiritual message. Priority aside, like many passages of scripture it carries both messages simultaneously. However many medieval commentators seem to prefer the spiritual or allegorical sense of passages of the Bible to their literal context. Evans in her discussion of allegory says this in regard to the medieval use the spiritual sense of a passage: "One of the values of having the spiritual sense at the exegete's disposal is that they make it possible to get around the difficulty that the literal sense is sometimes very opaque indeed, and that is one reason why it is inclined to dominate the spiritual with its crude obviousness. The literal sense can even be repugnant."[317] That certainly seems to be the case for Bernard and despite the amount of time he spends in discussion and commentary upon this love poem, he finds solace in the striking imagery and erotic language as representing solely the spiritual sense to which he ascribes it. As Evans has noted that allows him license in application without too much stirring up of the passions in his monastic listeners in an unfitting manner. Bernard underscores this point in his First Sermon on the Canticles regarding the subject matter he is embarking upon: "For it would be criminal presupposition on the part of imperfect souls to occupy themselves with such a sacred subject before the flesh has been tamed by discipline and subdued by the spirit,

---

[317] Evans, *Bernard*, 62.

and the vanity and cares of the world despised and abjured."[318]

In both his Commentary and Sermons, Bernard begins with the first words of the book of Solomon's poem, however he does not move in an expositional manner through the book. Rather he chooses select passages upon which to elaborate. In his *Commentary on the Song of Songs*, Bernard moves through the book in 43 sermons. Throughout his life he expands upon even this number, and his collected *Sermons on the Canticle of Canticles* number 86. Throughout, his concern is that his hearers take away the importance of a personal and mystical union with God. Love is the debt which owed from creature back to Creator, and the greatest goal of humanity must be a return to the bliss of intimate relationship with the divine for which they were created. Gilson elaborates upon Bernard's writings in saying: "A love of sufficient ardour is a kind of inebriation; and so it must needs be in order that the soul may have the mad audacity to aspire to the divine union."[319]

In this we see the underlying purpose of Scripture, which is to bring the reader to a place where a life of love for God is the natural result of its reading. The Bible is God's words and in so representing the divine nature represents the very wisdom which comes from God. Not just wisdom which comes from God, but in a personified sense becomes Wisdom, itself a representation of one aspect the divine nature. Bernard characterizes the personal relationship with the Word: "For it is an occupation full of sweetness and grace to contemplate the obscure mysteries of wisdom in Wisdom itself, a source of the greatest honor and glory that the effects

---

[318] *Sermons on the Canticle of Canticles*, First Sermon: On the Meaning of the Title: "Solomon's Canticle of Canticles".

[319] Etienne Gilson, *The Mystical Theology of Saint Bernard* (London: Sheed and Ward, 1955), 112.

produced by causes hidden in the Word of God should be revealed for the world's admiration by their ministry."[320] The voice of God speaks wisdom, and Wisdom herself becomes a representation of the divine wisdom who speaks to the reader out of the pages of Scripture. The Word of God speaks truth, and speaks the laws of God, which bring the penitent to their knees. Only in humility can the believer learn love, and only in humility can the believer live out the life of love for God, a life for which humanity had been created.

Gilson, in his commentary on Bernard, establishes three conditions by which humanity is able to meet the status and purpose for which they were created, that of union with the divine. First, humankind is capable of immediate and direct contact with God, therefore human beings must be capable of conceiving of God and of relating to Him. This is how human persons demonstrate that they are above the animals, for beasts cannot conceive of contact with God. Likewise angels exist in a state of constant contact with God and exist on the same spiritual plane, and have no choice but to worship God. Created humanity was given the choice and the ability to choose to worship, which is what the Creator desires. The second condition which must exist before the believer is able to experience mystical union is that the Spirit of God must penetrate our spirit. This action is accomplished by the intermediary effect of the Word of God, by which Bernard means the person of Christ. It is only through the actions of the God-man, as revealed in the Holy Scriptures, that the way of love between creature and Creator is reopened. The final condition which must be met is the believer must wish to go deeper in relationship than merely obedience or even piety. Rather the love of God opens up a means to the divine union which is characterized by the desire of the Bride for her Groom in the Song of Songs and

---

[320] *Commentary on the Song of Songs*, Sermon 19: The Loves of the Angels, S:3.

by the ultimate expression of that love which is to be permanently sealed in marriage. Gilson again: "In short, the love of God, when brought to this degree of intensity, has something of the character of heavenly beatitude, inasmuch as it is an end in itself, the possession of which dispenses with all the rest because it includes it."[321]

For Bernard, the state of bliss for which humankind was created, that condition which arises from a personal, interactional, relationship of love with the divine, is not merely a promise for the life beyond this one. It is attainable here on earth and in fact is the highest calling for the believer. Bernard uses a variety of word pictures to express this truth, most of which come from his exposition on the Song of Songs. Here Sommerfeldt states: "But the teaching behind all of them [word pictures] is the same: love is the perfection of the will, free to choose the good....Still more fundamentally, Bernard is sure that, in loving, one participates in the very being of God."[322] The purpose of Scripture then is to reveal the God who wishes to be loved, and to show the truth of the promise of a return to the created and intended blissful condition. Bernard has concern for those believers (primarily his fellow monks) who may not be able to see the deeper meaning of Scripture as he does himself. His concern in one of his final sermons on the Canticles is that his hearers will not understand the nature of the relationship between the Church and Christ, Bride and Groom, stemming from God's deep love for the Church.

> By what means, I ask, shall I be able to prove to
> them that the case is with the Spouse as I have

---

[321] Gilson, *Mystical Theology*, 111. I am particularly indebted in this section to Gilson, who outlines these conditions in pages 108-111 of the above mentioned work.

[322] John R. Sommerfeldt, *The Spiritual Teachings of Bernard of Clairvaux* (Kalamazoo, MI: Cistercian Publications, 1991), 100.

presented it to be, since they have not as yet discovered in their own experience anything like what I have described? But I will refer them to a witness whose testimony they are bound to accept. Let the read in thc Holy Book that which, because they cannot see it in the heart of another, they perhaps hesitate to believe....These my brethren are the words of God Himself, and it is not lawful for us to doubt them.[323]

Here we see outlined the underlying foundation as held by Bernard, that Scripture serves to the life of the believer. The Bible is God's words, which reveal to the reader His Word, the Son, and reveal Wisdom, who is the personification of God's wisdom. The believer, in fervent desire for God, turns to the words of the Bible to find God Himself revealed, the Groom who is the object of love and desire by the Bride, His Church.

Doctrine, Philosophy, and Theology

Aquinas begins his *Summa Theologiae* with the question of what the source of doctrine is. Upon what foundation do we build our Christian beliefs? In his refutations he states human beings should have no need of any knowledge beyond philosophical science, a subset of which he refers to as theology. Yet that knowledge is lacking for, as he endeavors to show throughout later parts of this work, human knowledge is fractured by virtue of the effect of original sin. Human beings cannot know God fully, and because of this fact more must be revealed about God than could be uncovered by human understanding of the sciences. He states in the very first questions of the *Summa Theologiae*: "It was necessary for man's salvation that there should be a

---

[323] *Sermons on the Canticle of Canticles*, Sermon LXXXIV: On Seeking God.

knowledge *revealed by God* besides philosophical science build up by human reason."[324] Thus general revelation does not bring human beings to a complete and salvific knowledge of God, although a limited knowledge of God is certainly garnered from creation. God has granted to human persons the ability to reason and to discover, an ability which is inherent to the *imago dei.* However, in order to understand beyond the visible requires two things: first God must reveal Himself to the seeker and second this revelation must be accepted by faith.[325] These two facets form for Aquinas the foundation of what he then calls "sacred science" which is that divinely initiated act of seeking for truth about God.

He goes on to establish sacred doctrine as a science, a consideration which unfortunately has been lost in our post-modern construct which relegates theology to the humanities. This was a key consideration is his day as well, for even in the earliest universities, Naples and Paris, a burgeoning movement was underway to treat philosophy, logic, and rhetoric as distinct from and receiving lower emphasis than law, mathematics, and the natural sciences. Even so, Aquinas refuses to differentiate sacred science from a practical science, for sacred doctrine includes both the speculative aspect and the practical. Aquinas points to Scripture as the source of doctrine and the foundation of sacred science when he states: "Because Sacred Scripture

---

[324] *ST,* I-I.1.1. Emphasis mine.

[325] Ibid. McInerny states this quite well: "There is, then, in man a threefold knowledge of things divine. Of these, the first is that in which man, by the natural light of reason, ascends to knowledge of God through creatures. The second is that by which the divine truth – exceeding the human intellect – descends on us in the manner of revelation, not, however, as something made clear to be seen, but as something spoken in words to be believed. The third is that by which the human mind will be elevated to gaze perfectly upon things revealed." Ralph McInerny, *A First Glance at St. Thomas Aquinas* (Notre Dame: University of Notre Dame Press, 1990), 64.

considers things precisely under the formality of being divinely revealed, whatever has been divinely revealed possess the one precise formality of the object of this science." [326] Min adds: "The first principles of theology are neither self-evident nor rationally demonstrable, as are those of other sciences; they derive from a higher science, the knowledge of God and the blessed revealed in Scripture....In this sense, divine revelation remains the principal source and the controlling norm and horizon of all theology."[327] In this way we can see Aquinas equates Scripture with divine revelation and establishes the authority of Scripture from its source in God Himself. Sacred doctrine may rely upon the wisdom of philosophers, as Aquinas himself does continuously and convincingly, and may further rely upon the doctors of the church who had come before and expounded upon Scripture. Yet, Aquinas unequivocally establishes the authority of Scripture to the development of sacred doctrine precisely due to its nature as God's revelation of Himself.

> Nevertheless, sacred doctrine makes use of these [extra-biblical] authorities as extrinsic and probable arguments; but properly uses the authority of the canonical Scriptures as an incontrovertible proof, and the authority of the doctors of the Church as one that may be properly used, yet merely as probable. For our faith rests upon the revelation made to the apostles and prophets who wrote the canonical books, and not on the revelation (if any such there are) made to other doctors.[328]

---

[326] *ST*, I-I.1.2.

[327] Anselm K. Min, *Paths to the Triune God: An Encounter Between Aquinas and Recent Theologies* (Notre Dame: University of Notre Dame Press, 2005), 21.

[328] *ST*, I-I.1.8.

Baglow shows how a modernist consideration that Thomas' acceptance of the authority of Scripture exhibits a pre-critical approach can be a weakness in understanding Thomist theology and philosophy as a whole. He informs us: "It is necessary to begin by asserting a well-established fact, namely, that Thomas sees Sacred Scripture and sacred doctrine as unified, being themselves phases of a broader dynamism of revelation."[329] Scripture and doctrine, likewise Scripture and knowledge of God, are intrinsically linked in that human reasoning requires God's revelation of Himself for the person to even know Him at all. Our initial exposure to God is through general revelation followed by a far deeper and more personal understanding of God through the specific revelation within Holy writ.[330] Baglow again expands upon this consideration: "The fact that the words of Scripture are human words makes them a *way* which the human mind can traverse; the fact that these human words contain divine revelation make them the medium of divine truth as well as salvation."[331] For Thomas the canonicity of Scripture is never debated, simply accepted from the outset as the authoritative

---

[329] Christopher T. Baglow, "Sacred Scripture and Sacred Doctrine in Saint Thomas Aquinas," in *Aquinas on Doctrine: A Critical Introduction,* Thomas G. Weinandy, Daniel A. Keating, and John P. Yocum, eds. (London: T&T Clarke, 2004), 2.

[330] Gilson sees Scripture as authoritative for doctrine and theology strictly on the basis of revelation, saying: "Sacred science or theology, then, has for its basis faith in a revelation made by God to those whom we call the apostles and prophets. This revelation confers upon them a divine and therefore unshakeable authority; and theology rests entirely on our faith in their authority." He then adds in a footnote: "Sacred teaching, or theology, therefore has no valid existence except as contained in sacred scripture....A non-biblical theology would be no theology at all." Etienne Gilson, *Thomism: The Philosophy of Thomas Aquinas*, trans. Laurence K. Shook and Armand Maurer (Toronto: Pontifical Institute of Medieval Studies, 2002), 11-12.

[331] Ibid, 3. Emphasis original.

underpinnings of doctrine.[332] Today's reader of Aquinas would do well to coalesce his philosophy with his theology, even as Aquinas himself stitched together Scripture with Platonic and Aristotelian logic so expertly as to establish Church doctrine for the next seven centuries.

By emphasizing Thomas-as-philosopher over Thomas-as-theologian, Pieper speaks disparagingly of Thomas' commentaries on the Bible, listing them as incidental to his "great works." By great works Pieper refers exclusively to the *Summas* and the Commentaries on Aristotle. Pieper argues: "The Biblical texts are for the most part historical utterances and not systematic logical treatises."[333] While this is certainly true, it is an error to believe that for Thomas the Bible had any place other than at the heart of his philosophy. Although God is transcendent, He becomes immanent by revealing Himself, He becomes knowable by speaking of Himself. While employing human language brings with it a naturally self-limiting factor, God chooses to reveal Himself in His words which are recorded for us in Scripture. Thus to understand what we may about God is to employ reason and logic, coupled with an acceptance of the words of Scripture as God's chosen methodology of self-revelation. O'Meara speaks to this juxtaposition in Aquinas: "Ultimately we must find human ideas, images, and languages for the divine.

---

[332] Min states so well: "The basic harmony between reason and faith makes it possible for theology to borrow philosophical arguments and principles for its own theological purpose of more clearly explicating the things of faith, provided, of course, that philosophy remains subject and secondary to the principles and light of faith, which should remain the ultimate controlling principle of theological reflection." Min, *Paths*, 25.

[333] Joseph Pieper, *Guide to Thomas Aquinas, 3rd ed.* (San Francisco: Ignatius Press, 1991), 98.

Aquinas' theory of speaking about God permits and encourages discussing God while at the same time affirming mystery and transcendence."[334] Smith similarly adds: "Revelation itself makes us more aware of the distinction between creatures and God precisely so that we may understand the truth about God's action, both in creation and in redemption. For that reason, Thomas argues, we are constricted by the language of Scripture and cannot go beyond it or set it aside in our theological reflections."[335] Thus study of Thomas' theology proper is best conducted within a construct of reason (logic and philosophy) balanced with belief (Scripture and revelation).

Law and Revelation

Thomas in the first part of the *Summa Theologiae* spends some space in discussion of Law. He references the Old Law (meaning the Old or First Testament of the Bible) and contrasts its purpose with that of the New Law (New Testament). For Thomas, the Old Law was given, despite its weaknesses, for several distinct purposes, all of which indicate that he saw Scripture as evidence of God's self-revelation. Some of the difficulties with the Old Law Thomas addresses immediately such as the fact that God is perfect, yet the Old Law is imperfect. Additionally God exists forever yet the Old Law was never intended to last forever. In countering these arguments against the validity of the Old Testament, Thomas shows the Old Law was given to show the transcendent goodness of God by establishing a standard that could not be met by the best of people. Some would

---

[334] Thomas F. O'Meara, *Thomas Aquinas: Theologian* (Notre Dame: University of Notre Dame Press, 1997), 93.

[335] Timothy L. Smith, *Thomas Aquinas' Trinitarian Theology* (Washington, D.C.: Catholic University of America Press, 2003), 11.

argue this is "not fair" of God to establish an unattainable standard, but the Old Law is given to show precisely the distance that exists between humans and God by virtue of original sin. At the same time the Old Law establishes ways of living which are beneficial to the larger community. Davies rightly elaborates: "The Old Law was given to help human beings at a time when they were unable to apply the precepts of natural law as they needed to be applied in particular circumstances."[336] Natural law is clearly shown to be subordinate to divine law, for human beings can reason about God and draw some concept of him from the natural order, but cannot receive divine revelation except through special revelation, that self-revelation which comes personally from God in the form of the written word. While reason can point us to God as the source of ultimate happiness, reason and observation of the created order can only bring one so far in regaining communion with God.

In this way, the Old Law served to establish for the ancient Jews a community of worship, one which was set apart from its neighbors by worship of the one true God and by its laws which required obedience and sacrifice. Thomas shows the Old Law served as "a kind of disposition, since by withdrawing men from idolatrous worship, it enclosed them in the worship of one God, by Whom the human race was to be saved through Christ."[337] Worship, intimacy, and a return to union with God could only (at the time) be achieved within

---

[336] Brian Davies, *The Thought of Thomas Aquinas* (Oxford: Clarendon Press, 1992), 257.

[337] *ST*, I-II.99.1. Hunt adds: "Although the ceremonies of the Old law could have been so instituted as to have had no figurative character, and no reference to the great truths of Christianity and of eternal life, God, in His infinite Wisdom, chose to give His people rites and ceremonies having not only a literal meaning, but also a figurative meaning. This served both to instruct his people, and thus to prepare the way for Christ and life everlasting, as well as to emphasize the absolute central character of Christ in all sacred history." Ignatius Hunt, *The Theology of St. Thomas on the Old Law* (Ottawa: St. Paul's Seminary, 1949), 27.

the structure of religious code which was set in place by the Old Law.[338] Thomas goes further to state: "It belongs to the divine law to direct people to one another and to God."[339] Additionally: "To the Divine law each man stands as a private person to the public law which he is subject. Wherefore just as none can dispense from public law, except the man from whom the law derives its authority, or his delegate; so, in the precepts of the Divine law, which are from God, none can dispense but God."[340]

This further paves the way for the giving of grace which could only come from God, and places humanity in need of that grace to overcome the sin which they cannot overcome on their own.[341] This would require the giving of a New Law, a law which established a new community. This community would not be bound by the norms and religious regulation of the previous Law, but would rather comprise a body of believers enlightened by special revelation and the ongoing presence of God Himself within each one. Davies feels that for Thomas the Old Law came before Christ to a specific group of people to prepare the way for the coming of Christ. It established law and God as the transcendent good, yet did not provide a means for truly overcoming the residual effects of original sin. Communion could not be attained by the giving of the Old Law for the reason that complete adherence to that Law was an unreachable goal for human beings.

---

[338] It must be noted here that Thomas did not see the Old Law as given to all people in all times, but specifically to the Jews to establish a model of community and to point to the time, place, circumstances, and socio-historical context in which Christ would be sent as the ultimate revelation of God.

[339] *ST*, I-II.99.4.

[340] *ST*, I-II.96.3. To be fair to the quotation we must note Thomas concludes this portion with the words: "…or the man to whom He may give special power for that purpose." I chose not to include that clause as it introduces a discussion of papal authority which is not germane to the current conversation.

[341] *ST*, I-II.98.3.

Davies provides the insight that "the precepts of the Old Law accord with reason and are good. But they cannot by themselves bring people to their final end. So Aquinas concludes the law is lacking."[342] In drawing this conclusion, it is natural that Aquinas should demonstrate the perfection of God as revealed in the New Law, and in so doing he begins with the twofold purpose of the New Law. First, "there is the chief element, that is, the grace of the Holy Spirit bestowed inwardly" and the second element is "the teachings of faith, and those commandments which direct human affections and human actions."[343] God sends His grace, which must enact belief in the heart of the penitent, and which is embodied in the Incarnation. Additionally God sends the third person of the Godhead to be present in the life of the believer, enacting grace in loving God and others as human beings were created to do from the beginning. Finally the New Law is composed by the initiation of the Holy Spirit in the Apostles writing of Holy Scripture, which stands as the authority for doctrine.

That is not say that for Thomas the New Law exists in distinction from the Old Law, rather that it is the fulfillment of the Old Law. The two are intrinsically tied together and the ceremonial practices of the Old Law point to the grace of the New Law. The precepts of natural law which are enumerated in the Old Law are maintained in the New Law which mandates love for God and for fellow human person. That ceremony is done away with is perfectly in keeping with the basis of the New Law for now God lives within the hearts of everyone and the ritual of the Old Law is no longer necessary. Thomas strikes this balance in saying: "The New Law does not void observance of the Old Law except in the point of ceremonial precepts [because they] were figurative of

---

[342] Davies, *Thought*, 259.
[343] *ST*, I-II.106.2

something to come. Wherefore from the very fact that the ceremonial precepts were fulfilled when those things were accomplished which they foreshadowed, this would mean that something is still to be accomplished and is not yet fulfilled."[344] For Thomas the fulfillment of the Old Law is evidenced in the person of Jesus Christ, who is the embodiment of the Godhead, present to earth and immanent in his physicality. Additionally grace is brought by the Incarnation and Davies adds "grace and the New Law go together for Aquinas since, in his thinking, the New Law involves people sharing God's nature."[345] The reader at this juncture should note that for Aquinas "the Old Law is like a pedagogue of children...whereas the New Law is the law of perfection, since it is the law of charity."[346] Loving God as human beings were intended to do is the result of the grace which motivates each believer toward God through faith, and the New Law perfects that faith through grace in the heart of the believer.

One final note as regards medieval hermeneutics is that Aquinas distances himself from both the hermeneutic of allegory which was evidenced by Bernard as well as from the heartfelt cries from the depths which were elucidated by Anselm. Rather even in his commentaries, Aquinas' systematic approach is evident, and he draws church doctrine from the pages of Scripture.[347] Thomas' reverence

---

[344] *ST*, I-II.107.2.

[345] Davies, *Thought*, 262. I differ with Davies in respect to his overemphasis on the Old Law being a written law and therefore being secondary to the New Law which is written on our hearts. Thomas' treatment of the New Testament throughout the *Summas* and *CoT* as well as his deep and systematic commentaries on the Scriptures indicate a reverence for the written word as the self-revelation of God, which cannot be discounted simply by virtue of the presence, or lack thereof, of the Holy Spirit.

[346] *ST*, I-II.107.2.

[347] As we have seen, Pieper and others decry this use of Scripture as forming the words of the Apostles around a false systematic construct. The same argument is often made today by those who dismiss systematic theology as being outside

for the Scriptures as the words of God is evident throughout his writings, and though he relies upon both neoplatonism and Aristotelian logic, his argumentation is never far from the words of Scripture. The authority of Scripture as the source of doctrine is systematized by logic, rather than a method which might come from the other way around. Baglow notes: "[W]e can reasonably assert that Thomas does display a close and fruitful identification of Sacred Scripture and sacred doctrine in his own articulation of the latter."[348] The reader of Aquinas would do well to understand his view of Scripture as God's self-revelation in both the Old and New Laws, a revelation which is enlightened by the words of God Himself in the Holy Spirit's presence within the individual.

---

the bounds of the manner in which the Scriptures are presented to us. To both commentators I make the same response: God has given the believer both reason and faith which work together to compel one toward a love of God and others, and into an understanding of God through both natural and special revelation. To systematize ones understanding of the Scriptures as they speak to the nature of God is to employ reasonable practices in an attempt to understand the nature of God. Thus Biblical theology and systematic theology are inherently linked.

[348] Baglow, *Sacred Scripture*, 16.

CHAPTER FIVE:
GOD REVEALED IN THE PERSON OF CHRIST

Anselm and the necessity of the Incarnation

"By what logic or necessity did God become man, and by his death, as we believe and profess, restore life to the world, when he could have done this through the agency of some other person, angelic or human, or simply by willing it."[349] With these words the magnificent doctor begins one of his most key works, the *Cur Deus Homo*. In asking the titular question of why God became human (a more literal phrasing of the question would be Why a God-man? or Why [the necessity of] a God-man?), Anselm embarks upon an investigation of the person of Jesus Christ which shows Him so plainly to be God Incarnate, and as such is the highest revelation of God Himself to the world. Using the form of a dialogue between teacher and student, Anselm argues against an unbeliever's outside viewpoint that God could have saved the human race from its fallen state in any other way, and establishes the logical necessity of the person and work of Christ.

Visser and Williams distinguish in Anselm's thought between the work of Christ and person of Christ showing that: "For Anselm, soteriology comes first; only when we understand what Christ must *do* can we understand what Christ must

---

[349] Anselm, *CDH*, 1.1.

be."[350] This becomes a key distinction of thought when one considers the introduction to *Cur Deus Homo* in which Anselm states clearly: "...human nature was instituted with the specific aim that at some stage the whole human being should enjoy blessed immortality."[351] Thus the Creator God began with a purpose for the human race of intimate relationship with Himself, and though creation began in perfection, God knew perfection would not last. He granted human beings true free decision-making, knowing that it would result in separation of humanity from God, for God's transcendent perfection cannot dwell with humankind's fallen and fractured state. He simultaneously embarked upon an ambitious plan to redeem humankind to Himself in eternity, but had to show Himself in some limited way to humanity so they might freely choose to love Him. Thus God revealed Himself in the person of Christ, who exercised His own free will to sacrifice Himself for humanity on the cross.

Boso, who was probably a fellow monk and close friend of Anselm, is cast in the role of the student in *Cur Deus Homo* and asks the key leading question to the beginning of the book. He requires an answer from Anselm to demonstrate the logic or necessity by which God Almighty took upon Himself the "humble standing and weakness of human nature."[352] This is the best starting point for understanding Anselmian Christology in that it demonstrates from the outset that restoration of humankind was required by God's very nature. His holiness and perfection could never collocate with the imperfect and damaged, and humanity was created for that purpose of relating. God owed it to Himself to find a way to restore fallen humankind and more

---

[350] Sandra Visser and Thomas Williams, *Anselm* (Oxford: Oxford University Press, 2009), 213. Emphases original.

[351] *CDH*, Preface.

[352] *CDH*, 1.1

so that means of restoration had to come from both God Himself and from a person in the created world. Anselm states: "The human race, clearly his most precious piece of workmanship, had been completely ruined; it was not *fitting* that what God had planned for mankind should be utterly nullified, and the plan in question could not be brought into effect unless the human race were set free by its Creator *in person*."[353]

If sin is failing to give to God what is owed (in the Norman feudal model of obligation) and humanity is unable to give what is owed, then a debt is left which separates humanity from God.[354] This is unfitting and God cannot relate with his creatures until the debt is satisfied. God is unwilling to simply cancel the debt, because restitution is owed to His holy self. Thus humanity must repay their own debt, and must in some enormous way cover the debt for all humanity in all times of history and future. This is obviously impossible outside of some divine impetus. Thus a God-man was required, one person who embodied the separate but co-equal attributes of the divine and the created. Jesus, the second person of the triune God "is true God and true man, one person in two natures and two natures in one person."[355] In Christ God became immanent to the world, and David Hogg so artfully captures the gist of the current work in the opening line of Chapter 6 of his work emphasizing the beauty of Anselm's theology: "In the *Cur Deus Homo* we see the plan of redemption unfold in all its beauty, harmony and fittingness as the transcendent God recreates and reorders

---

[353] Ibid, 1.4. Emphases mine.

[354] We may reconstruct this argument by restating a conversation between Anselm and Boso. What God demands from every rational creature, and every creature owes to God as a matter of obedience, is to maintain truth and righteousness unflinchingly in his way of life and in what he says. Because of sin this requirement of righteous life, which is placed upon humanity by virtue of its being created by God, cannot be met. Ibid, 1.9.

[355] Ibid, 1.8.

sinful humanity through the immanence of the incarnation."[356]

Additionally for God to be true to Himself, He could not coerce the God-man into sacrificing Himself. Rather this must be a combined act of will, the two natures determining the necessary course of action to meet the unpayable debt. Anselm drives home this point: "For the Father did not coerce Christ to face death against his will, or give permission for him to be killed, but Christ himself of his own volition underwent death in order to save mankind."[357] This outlines Anselm's argument for the necessity of the Incarnation in that humanity had to pay the debt they owed, yet this being impossible, God had to make it possible. A true man who was also God had to feely sacrifice Himself; in His human nature representing all fallen humanity and in His divine nature taking the punishment for sin and offering back to God a repayment of the debt through restitution.

This argumentation however is not without problems of its own, problems centering on the difficulties of juxtaposing the God-man's dual attributes and characteristics, such as how a sinless Man could be drawn from sinful humanity.[358] Sweeney shows: "More contradictions follow from the combination of divinity and humanity, a number having to do with the coexistence of necessity and freedom."[359] That is, how does the God-man both freely will to sacrifice Himself and simultaneously act in accordance with the necessity of action which was willed by God's immutable nature? This

---

[356] David S. Hogg, *Anselm of Canterbury: The Beauty of Theology* (Burlington, VT: Ashgate, 2004), 157.

[357] *CDH*, 1.9.

[358] Anselm's smaller work *De Incarnatione Verbi* (*On the Incarnation of the Word*) is largely a philosophical treatise outlining a logical response to many of these difficulties.

[359] Eileen C. Sweeney, *Anselm of Canterbury and the Desire for the Word* (Washington, D.C: Catholic University of America Press, 2012), 293.

difficulty is quite real, and Anselm spends some time in heavy philosophical and philological dialogue with Boso in order to rectify the two seemingly contradictory positions. David Hogg feels the apparent contradictions may be done away with if the reader remembers he or she is called to both reason and faith, and faith precedes and brings about understanding. While in some ways this frees Anselm from the necessity of "proving" his point on the grounds of pure logic, in other ways it muddies the waters where we do see Anselm making every effort to define the role of the God-man philosophically.[360]

Anselm's discussion of the necessity of the God-man becomes a form of theodicy, where if God had the power to redeem fallen humanity without the suffering of His Son, why would He not have chosen that avenue to enact *rectitudo*, whereas if He did not possess that power, He is not omnipotent. Sweeney makes the observation that Anselm argues humankind was made for happiness (both God's and their own) and perfect happiness cannot be found in this life of sin.[361] Further God in His holiness cannot abide with sin and there must be separation. Finally, "remission of sin is necessary for happiness" and forgiveness of sin through

---

[360] To this point Hogg states: "What this [necessity of belief] means for the reader is the *Cur Deus Homo* is thoroughly rooted in Christian presuppositions. Its arguments, its progression of thought, its context, are intended to be criticized from within that same context. Any attempt to shift the ground of examination, whether through anachronistic interpretation or modern philosophical speculation, will inevitably result in deracinating its constituent elements." Hogg, *Anselm of Canterbury*, 159. Ward seems to concur with this understanding to a certain extent. "In both the atonement theology of *Why God became Man* and here in the *Proslogion*, Anselm was not concerned to 'prove' anything in the modern sense....He was treating the doctrine of the atonement and the *Proslogion* as Eastern Christians treat an icon, as a way through, a way to be in touch with the reality that it represents in order to be changed by it." Benedicta Ward, *Anselm of Canterbury: His Life and Legacy* (London: SPCK, 2009), 25.

[361] Sweeney, *Desire for the Word*, 285.

mercy alone is unfitting.[362] The picture Anselm paints logically here is that God requires punishment for sin, desires to restore humanity, and is able to offer mercy after punishment. That punishment falls upon the only person it can, the only person who can bear the weight of the punishment for all humankind, Jesus Christ. Simultaneously, only a sinless human being can repay the debt for all humanity as well, a sinless human being who willingly and personally chooses to sacrifice Himself. The resultant *rectitudo* is the necessity for the God-man who must receive the punishment for sin and offer the mercy of God to all sinners.

Mercy and Revelation

In his prayer to Christ, Anselm cries out: "Lord Jesus Christ, my Redeemer, my Mercy, and my Salvation....Hope of my heart, strength of my soul, help of my weakness, by your powerful kindness complete what in my powerless weakness I attempt."[363] Here Anselm shows how the Incarnation is the only act which could bridge the divide between Creator and fallen creation. This act is an extension of God's nature. Anselm clearly shows in *Cur Deus Homo* the necessity for the redemption of humankind because of God's very nature. This necessity does not preclude the fact that this act of the work of Christ was an act of mercy as well. God's holiness demands *rectitudo,* demands restitution of the debt which must be paid to him, and as we have seen that debt must be paid by a human being for all humanity. Although this restitution is necessary for humankind to return to their created state and role, which God demands by virtue of His creative act, two determinative acts are required for this debt to be paid and God to receive what is owed Him. The first act

---

[362] *CDH*, 1.12.

[363] Prayer to Christ, *in The Prayers and Meditations of St. Anselm*, trans. Benedicta Ward, (Harmondsworth, UK: Penguin Books, 1973), 93.

is that of God's mercy being extended to rescue His fallen creation and the second act is the willful receiving of grace from God by one who so chooses freely to do so. Still, punishment for the unrequited indebtedness is required by God's holiness for "a sinner is bound not to be set free without punishment, except in the event that mercy pardons the sinner and frees him and restores him."[364]

If humankind is to be restored to a position of eternal bliss, the state for which they were created, sin must be eradicated. We have seen above that God's nature demands the absence of sin to commune with His creation, and God desires this communion. Humanity should desire this intimacy as well, for relating to God is the purpose for creation in the first place. God's mercy cannot be extended however until the debt is repaid; God demands satisfaction of the debt, which is owed Him, through the means we have seen Anselm outline in the section above.[365] Then humankind is able to reside in the state of bliss for which they were created, and God's relationship with his creatures is permissible. Anselm further states: "This state of bliss ought not to be given to anyone whose sins have not been utterly forgiven, and this forgiveness ought not to happen except on repayment of the debt which is owed because of his sin and which is proportional to the magnitude of his sin."[366]

In fact, it is a necessity for Anselm, employing the rules of logic, that humankind return to the state of bliss, for God requires this by His very nature of perfection.[367] He cannot create what cannot be returned to its intended state, so the

---

[364] *CDH*, 1.7.

[365] Anselm states: "God in His mercy saves mankind, when he does not forgive a person for his sin, if the person in question does not give back what he owes on account of the sin." *CDH*, 1.25.

[366] Ibid, 1.25.

[367] Ibid.

necessity of redemption is underscored. At the same time this necessity does not counter the fact that mercy must be seen as a free gift from God, freely accepted by the believer.[368] For God created humankind righteous in the beginning and indeed had communion with Adam and Eve in the garden. Their decision to disobey resulted in a separation from the Garden and from God's presence, which we have seen for Anselm is the nature of death.[369] Yet, Anselm indicates the majesty of God's mercy when God out of His transcendent greatness should satisfy his own requirement for justice in one act of giving God the Son, the embodied immanence of God, to earth. God the Son then becomes the payment for debt, and enacts *rectitudo*. Anselm confirms this: "What indeed, can be conceived of more merciful than that God the Father should say to a sinner condemned to eternal torments and lacking any means of redeeming himself, 'Take my only-begotten Son and give him on your behalf', and that the Son himself should say, 'Take me and redeem yourself.'"[370]

It is important to note the act of accepting God's mercy is not a one-time effect. Anselm shows how the life of faith requires the contemplative believer to live in certain ways which bring glory to God and demonstrate their devotion to God and gratitude for His mercy. As may be best seen in the *Prayers and Meditations*, Anselm demands of the believer a life of prayer, meditation, and service, that the grace of God may be reenacted daily in their life. The believer in this life once having accepted the gift of mercy and believed for salvation, continues to owe a debt of love to God. This debt is satisfied

---

[368] For an excellent discussion on Anselm and mercy as perceived by Thomas Merton, the great 20th century monk and philosopher, see Ryan Scruggs, "The 'One Merciful Event': Thomas Merton on Anselm's Cur Deus Homo", *The Merton Annual*, 2017.

[369] Anselm embarks upon this discussion in the first four chapters of Book 2 of *CDH*.

[370] *CDH*, 2.20

by penitence, prayer, and service. Anselm remains stricken by the sin nature he and all humanity have inherited and even knowing the merciful act of Christ on the cross, he continues to decry his own sinful nature and plead for continued mercy in his life. Mercy in this way comes not only from God the Father and God the Son, but from all the saints who imbue greater love of God in the life of the believer. He prays to St. Mary, the mother of Jesus: "I long to come before you in my misery, sick with the sickness of vice, in pain from the wounds of crimes, putrid with the ulcers of sin....I am so filthy and stinking that I am afraid you will turn your merciful face from me."[371] In his voice we hear echoed the cry of all sinful humanity, who, stricken by our sinfulness, reach out for mercy and restoration.

Bernard and the Majesty of the Incarnation

"The Son of the Most-High is born. The Son, begotten of God before all ages, is Incarnate! The Word is become an Infant! Who can sufficiently admire? And it is not a needless Nativity, a superfluous condescension of Infinite Majesty. Jesus Christ, the Son of God, is born in Bethlehem of Judea."[372] These words, taken from Bernard's first sermon on the Vigil of our Lord's Nativity form for us the starting point to grasp Bernard's Christology. In these sermons, Bernard outlines the three gifts of the Incarnation: salvation, unction, and glory, which we will explore in turn. These are the reasons the Incarnation was not superfluous, but rather necessary. Salvation is necessary because Adam, the first man, chose sin and in so doing damaged the *imago dei* for all future generations. Speaking of this insult to the image of God, Bernard says: "But in this world the likeness could nowhere reasonably be found, nay, rather the divine image

---

[371] First Prayer to St. Mary, in Ward, *Prayers and Meditations*, 107.

[372] *Sermons of Saint Bernard on Advent and Christmas*; Sermon III: On the Vigil of Our Lord's Nativity; Part 1: "On the Joy His Birth Should Inspire".

would here still lie filthy and defaced."[373] Gilson characterizes humanity's free choice as necessary for happiness, for which God created humanity to enjoy with Him. He states: "That is why, creating man in order to associate with him with His own beatitude, God created him with the gift of free will (*liberum arbitrium*), and it is chiefly on account of his freedom that man is the 'noble' creature, made to the image of God, and capable of entering into society with God."[374]

Bernard goes on, not only in this sermon but many others, to clarify the necessity of salvation through the Incarnation, enacted by a twofold work of Christ on earth. Jesus who is the full glory of God, co-equal with the Father in majesty, "manifested Himself, endowed with full power for the twofold work of restoring what was deformed and strengthening what was weak."[375] Christ, fully God and fully human, came to Earth to repair the *imago dei* and return humanity to the representation of God for which they were created. God was insulted by humankind's choice to sin, and humanity in turn was rendered unable to return to God the love which they were intended to offer in the beginning. This is the second aspect of the above statement, in that through the Incarnation, human persons are both returned to a glorious representation of the divine likeness, not in this world but in the next, and is simultaneously granted the strength in this world to offer back to Him the love which is required of them. Thus the work of Christ for Bernard is to restore the *imago dei* and in doing so to enable love in the believer through faith and willful obedience.

---

[373] *Concerning Grace and Free Will*, Ch. X.

[374] Etienne Gilson, *The Mystical Theology of Saint Bernard* (New York: Sheed and Ward, 1955), 47.

[375] *Concerning Grace and Free Will*, Ch. X.

For Bernard this love and obedience are required by nature of the very purpose for which humankind was created. In speaking of the fall of the angels, Bernard sees the necessity that they had to perish, "for the *love of the Father* and the *honour of the King* demand judgement."[376] This is followed by a statement on the purpose of creating humankind:

> For this cause He created men from the beginning, that they might fill those lost places, and repair the ruins of the heavenly Jerusalem....After man's fall, however, He created no other creature in his place, thus intimating that man should yet be redeemed, and that he who had been supplanted by another's malice might still by another's charity be redeemed."[377]

This is incredibly important to Bernardian theology in that the purpose of the redemption of humankind was to meet this unfulfilled love for the Father which is required to maintain the honor of the King. Gilson connects love and honor in Bernard as well, using an example that is repeated in the Sermons on the Canticles: "God requires that He should be feared as Lord, that He should be honoured as Father; but as Bridegroom He would be loved."[378] This is the relationship Bernard is building toward in his understanding of sin and the Incarnation, for it is only by the work of Christ that the Father may receive the honor which is His due, and which is demonstrated in the love which the creature returns to its Creator.

---

[376] *Sermons of Saint Bernard on Advent and Christmas*; Sermon I: On Advent; Part I: On the Advent of Our Lord and its Six Circumstances. Emphases mine.

[377] Ibid.

[378] Gilson, *Mystical Theology*, 137.

Returning to the three reasons for the Incarnation we must secondly examine unction. This term (Latin: *unctio*) was used in the Middle Ages and continues to be used in reference to the sacrament of prayer for the seriously ill or dying. It also speaks to a healing action and the influence of a potion to the body. With this in mind, Bernard employs the term here in a slightly different sense, that of healing humanity's free choice. By choosing to sin, Adam forfeited for all successive generations of humankind the ability to choose not to sin. Original sin is now passed down from generation to generation, but Christ through the Incarnation became the first and only human being who overcame this inability and chose to not engage in any sin while on this earth. The ability to choose to not give in to sin is a further reflection of the divine image, a reflection which, although lost, humanity was intended to bear from creation. Bernard goes on to indicate that through Christ now all people have been granted this ability as well, although in this earthly life it is only accomplished through the most austere giving of oneself to the contemplative lifestyle and adherence to God's will. Evans sees action and good deeds as complementary effects of contemplation, and as necessary to the believer living out their meditation on God in the world.[379] Bernard goes on to state: "Thus no longer will the man be the servant of sin, when he doeth not sin; from which indeed set free, he will now begin to recover freedom of counsel and to vindicate his

---

[379] G. R. Evans, *Bernard of Clairvaux* (Oxford: Oxford University Press, 2000), 131. For his fellow monks, Bernard emphasized that actions should not overshadow contemplation: "But it is of central importance to the life of monks, who are professed to the spiritual life, that they do not allow contemplation to be crowded out by daily life." *Sermons of Saint Bernard on Advent and Christmas*; Sermon I: On Advent; Part I: On the Advent of Our Lord and its Six Circumstances. Tamburello does not see a distinction in Bernard between active love which is love for the fellow man, and affective love which he equates with the contemplative lifestyle. "Bernard will insist on the complementarity of the two kinds of love. The person who is active in service will be a better contemplative, and vice versa." Dennis E. Tamburello, *Bernard of Clairvaux: Essential Writings* (New York: Crossroad, 2000), 127.

dignity, while he clotheth himself with a likeness befitting the diving image in himself, yea restoreth his ancient comely state."[380] Thus through the Incarnation, unction is performed on the will so that humanity may be returned to the state of acting out the divine image in which they were created.

The third and final purpose for the Incarnation, after salvation and unction, is glory. Humankind lost the glory of God which they initially reflected, yet, for Bernard, are able to return that glorious state, both in this life and in the next. The state of glory in this life is enacted in us by means of the Holy Spirit and not by any merit which any person may feel they have of themselves. He tells us: "For indeed, by sending us good thoughts, He preventeth us; by also changing our evil wills He joineth us to Himself through consent; and, by supplying to our consent the opportunity of performance, by means of our manifest work He that worketh in us maketh Himself known outwardly."[381] The state of glory is returned to the creature in the life after this by a combination of the three works of the Incarnation. Through salvation the distance between humanity and God is bridged, through unction the will is reformed to act in accordance with God's, and through consent to grace the believer in life and death is returned to a position of relationship with God, thereby fully reflecting His glory.[382]

For Bernard, Christ in the Incarnation reveals and embodies the Wisdom of God. He is the Word of God, and He is

---

[380] *Sermons of Saint Bernard on Advent and Christmas*; Sermon III: On the Vigil of Our Lord's Nativity; Part 1: "On the Joy His Birth Should Inspire".

[381] Ibid.

[382] That is not to say that the creature ever fully shares in God's glory. Tamburello clarifies: "Bernard does say that it is appropriate to admire God's majesty, but we can never share in it, for that would be tantamount to an essential union. Conformity to God's will brings us as close as we will get to God, and that is very close indeed." Tamburello, *Bernard of Clairvaux*, 118.

representative of the relationship God desires to have with His creature, that of the love between a Bride and Groom. Speaking of Christ as representative of all the Father's glory, Bernard says: "Just as the sea is the ultimate source of wells and rivers, so Christ the Lord is the ultimate source of all virtue and knowledge....Indeed in him are hidden all the treasures of wisdom and knowledge."[383] If humankind is to be returned to a state of right relationship with God, they must be able to understand Him. Understanding truth about God instills the fear of Him in the believer, which further brings the believer to acting out good works. These are the twin facets of repairing the *imago dei*: restoring the human mind and restoring the human will, which are both brought about by the Incarnation.[384] The importance of Christ as the Wisdom of God is seen in that He is our teacher. Christ as teacher of humanity brings this knowledge of God to the fractured mind and through faith and belief enables the ability to live rightly and in accordance with God's commands. Bernard again writes: "One may presume that Christ, the Wisdom of God, our unique teacher in heaven and on earth, although reaching everywhere because of his spiritual power, yet imparts a special light to these in particular on whom he is enthroned, and from that august rostrum teaches knowledge to angels and to men."[385]

---

[383] *Commentary on the Song of Songs*, Sermon 13: Our Thanksgiving and God's Glory.

[384] Bernard states this in his *Commentary on the Song of Songs*: "[The Wisdom of God] quickly perceives a delusive tinge in all that the world holds glorious, truly distinguishing between it and deeper truth. Moreover, it causes the fear of God and the observance of his commandments to be preferred to all human pursuits and worldly desires. And rightly so, for the former is the beginning of wisdom, the latter its culmination, for there is no true and consummate wisdom other than the avoidance of evil and the doing of good, no one can successfully shun evil without the fear of God, and no work is good without the observance of the commandments." Sermon 1: On the Title of the Book.

[385] *Commentary on the Song of Songs*, Sermon 19: On the Loves of the Angels, S:4.

Speaking of Christ and the Incarnation, Bernard states: "He disdained not to be as a slave, though Himself supreme Master; to be poor, though possessed of all; to be flesh, though Himself the Word of God; to be the Son of Man, although He was the Son of God."[386] Here he contrasts flesh with Word of God, for the spoken word is incorporeal, but Christ who was that Word to the world became human in order to best present God's message. A word is intangible, merely a spoken sign by which communication is made, yet Jesus took on humanity that God's words would be best preached, and more so became in Himself the sign of God's communication. In this was this purpose of the Incarnation as Word ties together with that of Wisdom, for in Christ the wisdom of God is revealed to humanity. By embodying in flesh the divine nature and the simultaneous fully human nature, Christ represented God to the world. More so, He represented God's desire for His creation, redeeming fallen humanity's reason and desire back to the Creator. Bernard shows his listeners: "He is the eternal Word of God, for the Word was made flesh."[387] And also: "Since man, on account of the flesh, could understand nothing but what was of the flesh, behold, the Word was made flesh that man might be able even by the flesh to hear and understand the things of the Spirit. O man, behold that wisdom which was heretofore hidden is shown forth in you!"[388]

We recall that relationship with God had to be conceivable by humanity, and God Himself must be made approachable. In Christ both of these are fulfilled, for God came down, condescending Himself to the fractured state, and revealed Himself and His communication to humankind. This is the

---

[386] Untitled fragment included in *On the Love of God*.

[387] *Sermons of Saint Bernard on Advent and Christmas*; Sermon IV: On Our Lord's Nativity; Part III: On the Place, Time and Other Circumstances.

[388] Ibid.

only way God becomes relatable to His creation. Separation from God, for Bernard, is misery, an agony from which the human frame cries for release, but is unable to attain. Union with God is the created purpose of humankind and relieves the misery which sin brought to human beings by as the necessary result of separation from the Father. The mercy of God is seen in the Incarnation, in that Christ, who is both God and human, is sent to provide relief from misery. Salvation then is just that, a taking away of sin and an enabling of humanity to be able to return the debt of love which is owed to the Creator. Returning the love of the Father is a choice, an act of humanity's redeemed free will. Sommerfeldt here states: "The process of restoration requires one's response to God's grace....The will responds to God as a direct result of God's gift of himself in Christ by the Spirit."[389] Bernard declares: "In truth, our tribulations, both of body and soul, are multiplied, but from the necessities of both we are delivered by Him Who saves the whole man."[390]

Christ demonstrates this perfect relationship of love for which human beings were created. Tamburello considers the highest sense or highest form of love to be loving God so totally we do not think of ourselves.[391] Bernard shows the depth of this love in saying: "'For the Father loveth the Son' and embraces Him with an infinite affection, as the Supreme His Co-Equal, the Eternal His Co-Eternal, the One His Only-Begotten. But not less for Him is the love of the Son, Who even died for the love of the Father."[392] God the Father and

---

[389] John R. Sommerfeldt, *The Spiritual Teachings of Bernard of Clairvaux* (Kalamazoo, MI: Cistercian Publications, 1991), 28.

[390] *Sermons of Saint Bernard on Advent and Christmas*; Sermon IV: On Our Lord's Nativity; Part V: On the Words "Blessed be the God and Father of our Lord Jesus Christ".

[391] Tamburello, *Bernard of Clairvaux*, 85.

[392] *Sermons on the Canticles*; Sermon VII: On the Kiss of the Mouth Interpreted of the Holy Spirit.

God the Son love each other in a state of eternal bliss, and Christ in coming to earth embodies for the believer the relationship of love for God to which he or she is called.

Finally we would be remiss in our consideration of Bernardian Christology to leave by the wayside his sermons on the mysteries of the Incarnation.

> Let us with the Apostle [referencing Luke's story of the Advent] consider how great He is Who comes….He is the Son of the Most High, and consequently a coequal with Him. Nor is it lawful to think that the Son of God is other than coequal with His Father. He is coequal in majesty; He is coequal in dignity. Who will deny that the sons of princes are princes, and the sons of kings kings?[393]

This beautiful statement on Christ's divinity and the condescension required to leave heaven and become fully human for a time, speaks so eloquently to both the transcendence and immanence of God as seen in His Son. Bernard goes further to indicate the purposes of the Incarnation to which we have alluded above: "Take courage, you who were lost: Jesus comes to seek and save that which was lost. Ye sick, return to health: Christ comes to heal the contrite of heart with the unction of His mercy. Rejoice, all you who desire great things: The Son of God comes down to you that He may make you the co-heirs of His kingdom."[394]

In this way we see the immanence of God into the world in the person of His Son, who desires to restore humanity to the divine union with God which was damaged by sin. He

---

[393] *Sermons of Saint Bernard on Advent and Christmas*; Sermon I: On Advent; Part I: On the Advent of Our Lord and its Six Circumstances.

[394] *Sermons of Saint Bernard on Advent and Christmas;* Sermon III: On the Vigil of our Lord's Nativity; Part I: On the joy His birth should inspire.

wishes to heal humanity's fractured reason and will through mercy which enables the human person to live by God's commands in this life, and receive His glory in the next. The fallen creation is restored by the Son to the position for which they were created, co-heirs of the kingdom of God who live in a state of eternal bliss, saturated by the purest love for God. This for Bernard is the purpose of Christ coming to earth, the reason for the Incarnation, and the evidence of the highest form of God's self-revelation to His creation.

God's Choice beyond Necessity

Aquinas begins the fourth section of the *Summa Theologiae* as he always does, with an objection: "It would seem that it was not fitting for God to become incarnate. Since God from all eternity is the very essence of goodness, it was best for Him to be as He had been from all eternity." [395] That is to say that it would appear that for God to become embodied in any way which is not indicative of His eternally transcendent essence would be beneath Him, and show God as less than He truly is, since "God and flesh are infinitely apart."[396] Additionally he shows that it does not seem fitting that "He who surpassed the greatest things should be contained in the least."[397] It is important to note here that he does not say it is outside the bounds of logic or necessity, rather that these things are not seemly, fitting, or to put it another way, they do not make sense to our observation.

Yet there is more to the incarnation than God merely becoming in a lesser form than that in which He always exists, more than His putting aside of greatness to become the least, although both of these things are certainly true. In answering his objections, Aquinas indicates rather: "It would

---

[395] *ST*, III.1.1

[396] Ibid.

[397] Ibid.

seem most fitting that by visible things the invisible things of God should be made known," and further that "it belongs to the essence of the highest good to communicate itself in the highest manner to the creature."[398] In short it is proper that the Creator should reveal Himself in an understandable way to His creation, and that they may know Him or what they can of Him.[399] What is seemly and most fitting about the Incarnation is that God's self-revelation became progressively more understandable and relatable. Just as we saw that God's power and creative majesty may be known from general revelation, and a salvific knowledge of God may be drawn from Scripture, by God becoming embodied in a human person His nearness and redeeming love may be known personally.

Aquinas further answers his own objections as to the essence of God in stating that God's essence was unchanged in His taking on of mortal flesh. God's spirit essence remains for all eternity, but in the incarnation God merely takes on a form which may be relatable to human beings. Thomas draws from Augustine to show: "The mystery of the incarnation was not completed through God being changed in any way from the state in which He had been from eternity, but through His having united Himself to the creature in a new way, or

---

[398] Ibid.

[399] Pieper feels that for Thomas a discussion of the incarnation is a culmination of an argument that things, all things, are good not evil. They are inherently good because they were created by the God who is the highest expression of goodness. This is in contradistinction to an argument from the monastic orders of his day who sought to withdraw from the world with all of its evil and temptations. As a Dominican, it would seem most fitting to Thomas to be part of the world, to minister within it and not to withdraw behind the cloister walls. Pieper goes on to show Thomas "differed with the radical, secularistic worldliness of heterodox Aristotelianism by the determinedly theological foundation he gave to his ideas; he justified his worldliness by the theology of creation and by the strictly 'theological' theology of the Incarnation." Josef Pieper, *Guide to Thomas Aquinas* (San Francisco: Ignatius Press, 1991), 132.

rather through having united it to Himself."[400] This statement is key to Thomist Christology in that God desired a return to the intimacy between Himself and His creation in the Garden, even though He knew at the moment of creation that the First Persons would choose the way they did. And since God cannot change His essence to unite with human beings He had to bring them to Himself. This for Thomas is the foundation upon which all of the incarnation is built, that God chose to make a way to bring human beings back into the right standing with God in which they were created.

That such a way needed to be enacted was not a surprise to the Creator. God in His infinite wisdom knew that His creation would choose to act out of self-determination and in so doing would reject the relationship with God in which they thrived at the beginning. God in His providence knew from the beginning that He would bring into the world a means by which humankind could be restored. O'Meara so fittingly and poetically speaks to God's continued immanence to the world, even after His creation had become fractured for all posterity. He says: "The universe is not a hospital or junk-shop where a god is a sympathetic nurse or a defective machine. A god who can only watch and not weep is not divine. God loves, creates, sustains people on earth, but God's vison and life are much broader than the limits of humanity in this solar system."[401] This God, in His wisdom and providence, desires a return to the relationship for which humanity was created.

In opposition to Anselm, who felt the Incarnation to be a logical necessity based on the requirements which God had set in place for His honor to be restored, Aquinas shows two sides of the same coin in regards to necessity. On one hand

---

[400] *ST*, III.1.1.

[401] Thomas O'Meara, *Thomas Aquinas: Theologian* (Notre Dame: University of Notre Dame Press, 1997), 103.

Thomas feels the incarnation be a necessity and on the other he shows how it was not. The argument against is that one definition of necessity is when a certain end cannot exist without the cause. In that case the cause is necessary for the outcome. On the other hand, we use similar terms of necessity "when the end is attained better and more conveniently, as a horse is necessary for a journey."[402] This is to say that for God, who is omnipotent, no one way was necessary for He can do all things, and could have redeemed fallen humanity in a different way. However He chose to do so in a manner which most effectively fulfilled His own commitment to His creatures and in that way "it was necessary that God should become incarnate for the restoration of human nature."[403] Thus the best lens to perceive a Thomist necessity for the incarnation is that of God revealing Himself in a manner which would most efficaciously meet humankind at their level and in compatibility with human essence.[404]

Though he differs from Anselm in terms of necessity and the honor that is owed to God, Aquinas neatly sums up the *Cur Deus Homo* in two paragraphs. He shows that satisfaction for the sin of humankind cannot be made by a mere person, for no one person can represent the sin of all humankind.

---

[402] *ST*, III.1.2.

[403] Ibid.

[404] Legge shows in his excellent section on the incarnation that Christ as the Form of Image represented the highest expression of the *imago dei*, which was fractured in humanity by original sin. Further in this way, Christ is not merely the highest moral example to us, although He is that, He is also the exemplar cause and agent of our restoration. "In sum, the incarnate Image (1) *demonstrates* in all that he does and suffers what a perfect human life is, lived as the image of God; (2) he *becomes the way* for our return, inasmuch as we conform our lives to what he lived in the flesh; and (3) through what he does in the flesh, he also *accomplishes* our salvation and *acts* to conform us to himself (the latter, above all, by giving us the Holy Spirit)." Dominic Legge, *The Trinitarian Christology of St. Thomas Aquinas* (Oxford: Oxford University Press, 2017), 96. Emphases original.

Likewise the goodness of one person cannot "be made up adequately for the harm done to the whole of nature."[405] No created person is adequate for the task of representing all sin and all goodness and all sacrifice in a manner which would be acceptable to attain satisfaction for sin. Thomas points out:

> A sin committed against God has a kind of infinity from the infinity of the Divine majesty, because the greater the person we offend, the more grievous the offense. Hence for condign satisfaction it was necessary that the act of one satisfying should have an infinite efficiency, as being of God and man....And forasmuch as every imperfect presupposes some perfect things, by which it is sustained, hence it is that satisfaction of every man has its efficiency from the satisfaction of Christ.[406]

The incarnation points to the transcendent essence of God even through His taking on of human form, and the act of satisfaction for sin shows the greatness of God-in-flesh and His ability beyond that of mortals to take on the sin of all fallen humanity. The incarnation did not change God's immutable and transcendent nature, it merely clothed the divine nature in a way which would be understandable by human reason and relatable to the human soul. Thomas so simply and brilliantly shows God chose the means of the incarnation to draw us back to Himself, even though we had fallen so far away. God wanted us to know more of Him, and so He became immanent to our world in the most poignant way, that communion may be restored.

---

[405] *ST*, III.1.2
[406] Ibid.

The Threefold Role of Christ

A further study of Thomist Christology may be pursued through an understanding of the roles or purposes of the incarnate Son of God. We see Christ in Aquinas as fulfilling the roles of exemplar, enactor, and emissary and by exploring each in turn we will examine the strands of the incarnation and what it means.

Aquinas indeed set the stage for this view in stating the suitability of the incarnation is situated in original sin.[407] Sin was perpetuated from the beginning in the Garden as the First Persons chose to act outside God's explicit directions. God in His sovereign justice excluded them and their posterity forever from the Garden, lest they also eat from the tree of life and live forever in their state of perpetually sinning against God. At the same time He enacted law, both natural law and the Old Law in order to show human beings the standard to which they can never measure up. God chooses not to override our free will and gives everyone the ability choose, however the effect of original sin continues to act within the individual to cause them to both choose wrongly and be unable to choose otherwise. Christ is the *exemplar* of natural law and the Old Law, for He was able to live fully human in this life without giving in to sin.[408] For Thomas this is because His fully human nature was subject to original sin, but this was countered by the fact that His divine nature was not. Therefore He was given from birth a divine grace which enabled him not to sin, although his human nature desired to do so as much as ours do. Of this Thomas states:

---

[407] *SCG*, 4.50

[408] Aquinas adds to this argument in depth in the *Summa Contra Gentiles*, with specific chapters addressing various fallacies which had surfaced within Church tradition. Some of these heretical errors claim that Christ possessed a human body but not a divine nature (Photinus), that God's divine nature did not truly take on human form but rather existed as a kind of phantasm (Manicheans), or that Christ had no soul (Arians), among others. *SCG*, 4.29ff.

"[Christ] did not receive human nature from Adam as an agent although He did receive it from Adam as from a material principle."[409] That is to say that unlike the rest of humanity, Christ's human nature was derived from the First Parents in the sense of his physical body, but not effectively as drawing its sin nature from the same source. This was because grace was enacted first in Christ's humanity, having the effect of stripping original sin from his nature and enabling sinlessness, although without mitigating the temptations of the flesh. Thus Christ is the exemplar of following the Old Law.

The New Law however sets a different standard and is enacted in our lives by the Atonement, which is only brought about by the incarnation. Thomas tells us: "He properly atones for an offense who offers something which the offended one loves equally, or even more than he detested the offense. But by suffering out of love and obedience, Christ gave more to God than was required to compensate for the offense of the whole human race."[410] The act of the Atonement enabled the possibility of humankind being restored to relationship with the Creator, possibility but not certainty, for human beings still must choose to accept the gift of grace and the Holy Spirit in right living in this life. But a New Law is in effect which allows human beings to not be measured by the same standard, the impossible standard of the Old Law, but rather because the standard has already been met, to receive grace. Dauphinais and Levering touch on Thomas' reference to divine law as both "the expression of divine Wisdom" and "the wise order of creation."[411] This Wisdom is seen both in God's establishment of the Old Law

---

[409] *SCG*, 4.52.9.

[410] *ST*, III.48.2.

[411] Michael Dauphinais and Matthew Levering, *Knowing the Love of Christ* (Notre Dame: University of Notre Dame Press, 2002), 63.

and Christ's fulfillment of it, bringing into effect the New. This New Law stems from an act of grace, which is counter to natural law and original sin. Christ *enacts* grace within each of us, first by his performance of the act of Atonement, which as we saw above, could only have been accomplished by a person embodying the human and divine. He further enacts grace within us by sending the Holy Spirit, about which we shall have much to say in the next chapter. Christ does not enact God's providence which from the beginning sustains all things. Dauphinais and Levering again: "Divine providence extends to all of creation, but especially to humans. Gods providence orders us to our end principally by means of law and grace."[412] Christ extends God's providence into the realm of sustaining our intimacy with Him, through a new covenant. Christ not only exemplified the Old Law and lived it perfectly, but He is the *enactor* of grace thereby bringing about the New Law.

Finally Christ is the *emissary*, the ambassador of God's love. An emissary is one who goes between two nations, carrying messages, bringing peace out of war, and enacting agreements. Original sin placed such a gulf between creature and Creator that it could not be spanned by the creature. However God in His holy and eternal essence could not become anything less to bridge the gap. The only answer to this conundrum was to send an emissary, a mediator, who could be representative of both the divine essence and human nature, and for that mediator to willingly sacrifice Himself as satisfaction of the unpayable debt.[413] Thomas

---

[412] Ibid, 62.

[413] McInerny sums this up nicely: "By Original Sin the race had fallen from a primordial innocence and bliss. God promises a redeemer and at long last, in the fullness of time, Christ is born, true God and true man. His sacrifice is the redemption of mankind, making possible an eternal happiness with God. Christ is the way, the truth, and the life. An eternal happiness with God is our destiny." Ralph McInerny, *A First Glance at St. Thomas Aquinas* (Notre Dame: University of Notre Dame Press, 1990), 157.

tells us: "Properly speaking, the office of a mediator is to join together and unite those between whom he mediates: for extremes are united in the mean...consequently, Christ alone is the perfect Mediator of God and men, inasmuch as, by His death, he reconciled the human race to God."[414]

Reconciliation is the mean between the two parties, the middle ground, but it is also the goal. Two parties who are estranged or at odds cannot communicate directly, but only through the mediator. However those who have been reconciled to each other are enabled to not only communicate freely and directly, but in fact share a relationship which would be impossible otherwise. As Anselm described, the God-man is the only one who can accomplish reconciliation as the emissary between God and humanity. Aquinas builds upon Anselm and Augustine in stating: "Christ had beatitude in common with God, mortality in common with men."[415] In sharing the divine nature, Christ had the authority to act on behalf of the Father, essentially representing the divine party in the mediation. Additionally as a human person He possessed a shared nature with humanity, thereby allowing Him to represent the mortal party at the table. His authority over sin is by virtue of His divine nature and His satisfaction of the debt of sin is by virtue of His humanity coupled with His willingly giving of Himself. Thomas concludes: "Although it belongs to Christ as God to take away sin authoritatively, yet it belongs to Him, as man, to satisfy for the sin of the human race. And in this sense He is called the Mediator of God and men."[416]

---

[414] *ST*, III.26.1

[415] Ibid.

[416] Ibid.

CHAPTER SIX:
THE HOLY SPIRIT AND GOD'S SELF-REVELATION WITHIN THE INDIVIDUAL

The Necessity of Tri-unity

Anselm in speaking of the Holy Spirt is primarily concerned with two major themes. First is an understanding of the triune God and why He must exist as three persons but one God. Second, he spends a great deal of argumentation addressing whether the Holy Spirit proceeds from the Father alone or from both Father and Son. The inclusion of the *filioque* clause into the Nicene Creed, and its subsequent controversy had already been a point of contention between Eastern and Western churches and came to a head in the Great Schism of 1054.[417] Both churches anathematized each other over the question of its inclusion, a move which in 1054 was primarily politically motivated. Several subsequent councils were held to continue the discussion and work to bring healing, but East and West would never again be one church. One such council, held at Bari in 1098, was presided over by Pope Urban II, who had appointed Anselm as special counsel to address in detail the theology in question. The result of the council of Bari was a failure on the one hand to attain capitulation from the Eastern Church representatives. Yet it was a success on the other hand for the Roman Church

---

[417] Latin: "…and the Son". Accepted as an addition to the Nicene Creed by most Western fathers but its inclusion was disputed by most Eastern Church leaders who felt it should remain that the Holy Spirit and the Son proceeded from the Father alone.

to effect a stabilization of Rome's influence over the Norman lands of France and North Italy, a matter which was of extreme importance to Anselm on a personal level.[418] This dispute with the Greek Church and the philosophical and Biblical discourse which Anselm brings to bear in his argumentation afford an excellent study in their own right, but speak little to the current topic. Rather we will focus our attention more closely upon Anselm's writings on the persons of the Godhead. Here we see Anselm establishes an orthodox view of the three-in-one nature of God, where each person is unique and distinct from the others, and all three are God in essence, and there is one God.

In *On the Incarnation of the Word,* Anselm lays out his position regarding the nature of the Trinity, showing that it is not only possible but necessary to see God as existing in three persons, but that there are not three gods.[419] Further God is not the combination of the three persons, rather God is God, and exists in three distinct persons, each of whom is co-equally God.[420] Anselm uses Platonist reasoning to show that a being is higher if composed of parts yet can simultaneously be considered simple in and of itself. This being is God, who exists as Father, Son, and Holy Spirit. In the *Proslogion,* the Holy Spirit is shown to be the love that

---

[418] Nathan Amerson, "Anselm Among the Normans: Spiritual Leader or Exile?", Presented at the 2019 conference of the Atlantic Medieval Society, Memorial University, St. Johns, Newfoundland, Canada. Anselm in 1098 had been exiled from his position as the Archbishop of Canterbury by William II (or Rufus), son of William the Conqueror over disputes with the king regarding taxation of church lands and lay investiture. He was allowed to return only when William Rufus was on his deathbed.

[419] The entirety of this work is to dispute a twisted version of his argument which had been poorly represented by a fellow monk, Roscelin.

[420] Roscelin argues: "No single person is God; rather, God is the product of the three things. Therefore, the Father is not God, the Son is not God, the Holy Spirit is not God, since we should predicate God only of the three mentioned together." *On the Incarnation of the Word*, S:4.

exists between the Father and Son.[421] Just as for Anselm the Word of God is personal and is the Son, so the Love between God the Father and the Son is personal and is the Spirit. In forming his argumentation for the highest good being found in the nature of God Himself, he states: "You are this good, O God the Father; this is Your Word, that is to say, Your Son....Love, one and common to You and to Your Son, that is the Holy Spirit proceeding from both."[422]

It is upon the personal nature of the Holy Spirit which we wish to concentrate in this section. In *On the Virgin Conception and Original Sin*, Anselm uses a number of word pictures to capture the nature and purpose of the Holy Spirit working in the created world. First, the Holy Spirit is a teacher, and "by the Holy Spirit the hearts of men are taught things which they knew neither from themselves nor from any other creature."[423] Second, the Holy Spirit worked miraculously in the virgin to cause and empower the conception of the God-man: "From her the Holy Spirit willed and was to effect the conception and birth of the Son from whom the Spirit should proceed."[424] Further, "The Holy Spirt and the Power of the Highest effected the miraculous propagation of a man from a virgin woman."[425] For Anselm this effective power of God in the person of the Holy Spirit working within the Virgin Mary is of key importance. Although Anselm does not hold that she was also sinless, by virtue of the power of the Holy Spirit in the miracle of

---

[421] This theme will be further explored below in Bernard's interpretation of this concept.

[422] *On the Incarnation of the Word*, S:4. Note here the connection to God as the highest good is drawn from *Timaeus*, 29e. Also the reader should note the proto-argumentation for inclusion of the *filioque* clause in his statement on procession.

[423] *On the Virgin Conception and Original Sin*, S:11

[424] Ibid, S:18.

[425] Ibid, S:23.

conception Christ's divine nature was protected from the perjury of sin. Even so His human nature retained its free will and predilection toward the sinful nature bestowed by Adam. It is by the power of the Holy Spirit that Christ was able to live a life in this world, fully divine and fully human, and yet never sin, thereby presenting the perfect sacrifice to God and enabling *rectitudo* for humankind.

Knowledge and Love

Anselm, in the early pages of *On the Procession of the Spirit* observes: "Something indeed happens to those who receive the Holy Spirit."[426] He shows here the Holy Spirit is given or sent to creatures, meaning humankind. It is this gift which enables faith to reason, and which reveals the unapproachable God to fallen humanity. Coupled with God's revelation in the Scriptures, the Holy Spirit speaks into the mind and heart of the believer teaching them things they would not otherwise be capable of knowing. Visser and Williams show that for Anselm: "Such spiritual formation enables the Christian to 'experience' the truth of Christian doctrine."[427] Knowledge of God is not possible without His stooping to our level and giving us the ability to comprehend His nature. Shannon adds: "The inaccessibility of God means that we cannot know God as God is in the divine self. We can only catch glimpses of God in the 'images' of God that come under our experience."[428] The self-revelation of God is brought home to us by the teaching of the Holy Spirit through the Word of God in the Scriptures and in the revealed person of Christ. It is because the Holy Spirit is co-equally God with the Father and the Son that He is able to

---

[426] *On the Procession of the Spirit*, S:2.

[427] Sandra Visser and Thomas Williams, *Anselm* (Oxford: Oxford University Press, 2009), 20.

[428] William H. Shannon, *Anselm: The Joy of Faith* (New York: Crossroad, 1999), 105.

reveal God to humanity. Drawing from the Gospel of John, Anselm writes:

> The Lord also says of the Holy Spirit to the Apostlcs, 'And when the Spirit of Truth has come, he will teach you all truth'[John 16.13], as if the Holy Spirit should be the one who teaches all truth, although he teaches all truth neither apart from the Father nor apart from the Son. For he does not teach all truth by reason of the fact that he is Spirit of someone, namely, the Spirit of the Father and the Son, but by reason of the that the Holy Spirit is one with the Father and the Son, that is, by reason of the fact that he is God.[429]

In this way we see Anselm speaks again of the Holy Spirit as the teacher, the one who reveals the Father and the Son, by virtue of his co-equality with them. God is able to overcome the fallen reason of humanity and reveal Himself by the action of the real and present person of the Holy Spirit in the world.

Further the relationship between the persons of the Godhead is first that they know each other. This knowledge of God, in His three persons, is affected in the mind of the believer by the Holy Spirit. In consideration of God's transcendent and immanent nature, Visser and Williams point out: "Because God is that than which nothing greater can be thought, he is both present to Anselm's mind and immeasurably distant from it. He both inspires Anselm's search and frustrates it, resisting any easy resolution but promising ultimate fulfillment."[430] Where Christ as the God-man is the bridge between a spirit God and a body-bound humanity, the Holy

---

[429] *On the Procession of the Spirit*, S:11.

[430] Visser and Williams, *Anselm*, 24.

Spirit is the bridge between God's distant self and His immanently relatable self. God is revealed to the mind which is affected to reason by faith through the person of the Holy Spirit.

For Anselm it is clear that the rational mind of the created person is a representation of God's very nature. The *imago dei*, although fractured by sin, continues to demonstrate in the creature a sample of what finds its highest and greatest expression in God. God created humankind with the ability to reason so that humanity might find God through His revelation of Himself. In the *Monologion* he states: "The ability to be conscious of, to understand and to love that which of all things, is greatest and best - no other gift bestowed on rational creation is conceivably as excellent of as similar to the supreme wisdom. No other created trait so betrays the image of its Creator."[431] To be able to conceive of God and to rationally articulate His existence is in fact an extension of God in His creature, a person's reason and rationality represents the highest reason and rationality which is only found in God. As we have seen, however, even this highest expression of God's creation, humanity itself, is damaged and exists in a state of being unable to find God even through His own self-revelation, unless the Holy Spirit acts upon the individual. Without the Holy Spirit, humanity would not know God. This ability to know God is, in Anselm's thought, a gift, in fact the greatest gift that has been given to the created order. Without God's self-revelation in the person of the Holy Spirit working in a person's mind, this gift could not be received.

Of the role of rationality in creation Anselm reveals: "To be able to be conscious of, understand and love the supreme good is its most momentous ability. And therefore the most

---

[431] *Mono*, S;67.

momentous debt that it owes its Creator is to want to be conscious of, understand and love the supreme good."[432] Just as the relationship between the persons of the Godhead is predicated upon the most intimate knowledge of each other, so the relationship that exists between them is love. Humankind was created to both know God and to love God but lost the ability to do so without God's granting us the presence of Himself to evoke that love within us. In the *Monologion*, Anselm breaks this argument down by parts: the supreme spirit loves itself, the Father and Son love each other equally, their love itself is as great as the supreme spirit is, their love in fact *is* the supreme spirit, love plus the Father plus the Son equals one spirit, thus the Holy Spirit is both a person of the Godhead and is the love that exists between the persons of the Godhead. This brings us full circle to the discussion in the paragraph above where just as humankind was created to be rational, so too they were made to love. Again he states: "It is as patently obvious, therefore, as it can be, that the rational creature is made for this purpose: to love the supreme essence above all other goods (insofar as the supreme essence is, after all, the good above all other goods."[433] Further, just as sin disrupted the created order and a person's reason must be acted upon by the Holy Spirit to understand God, so too our love must be acted upon by the Holy Spirit. If the love that exists between the persons of the Godhead is the Holy Spirit itself, so too the love that exists between the creature and the Creator is the Holy Spirit as well. Without the presence of this person in our lives, human beings would be unable to fulfill their purpose in being created and would be unable to repay the debt of love which is owed to the Creator.

---

[432] Ibid, S:68.
[433] Ibid.

It is fitting here to note that in none of Anselm's prayers does he address the Holy Spirit directly. His consciousness of sin and of humanity's inability to repay the debt owed to God drives his prayers and meditations, and Anselm vividly portrays the creature's inability and loss due to sin. Indeed this theme of love and loss of love is threaded through his prayers. This is why he cannot pray directly to the Holy Spirit; for the Spirit is the love that is lost and he must receive an infusion of that love from a third party. He desires Mary, who is closest to God by virtue of being the mother of Christ, to extend grace which allows the penitent's love for her to be transferred in love to God. Anselm's love is not enough to pay the debt, but he hopes by loving Mary his love for her will be taken as love for God. He prays to the great lady: "In my heart I know and worship you, love you and ask for your affection, not because of my imperfect desires, but because it belongs to your Son to make and to save, to redeem and bring back to life."[434] Anselm's prayers to Mary are unique in this way because he sees that only Mary of all people could love God with a perfect love, the love of a mother. Thus because she is closest to God and alone perfectly loved God, she is able to extend grace to fallen humanity to empower the love which they also wish to give to God. Conscious of his inability, in his prayer to Mary he says, "My tongue fails me for my love is not sufficient."[435] He goes on to indicate how mercy and grace may be extended from Mary herself and he wishes to be better enabled to love. Again he pleads: "Mary, I beg you, by that grace through which the Lord is with you and you willed to be with him, let your mercy be with me. Let love for you always be with me, and the care of me always be with you."[436] Returning to the

---

[434] Third Prayer to Mary, in *The Prayers and Meditations of St. Anselm*, trans. Benedicta Ward (Harmondsworth, UK: Penguin Books, 1973), 116.

[435] Ibid.

[436] Ibid, 121.

unpayable debt of love which is owed to the Creator, Anselm concludes the third prayer to Mary by asking that she enable love together with Christ.[437] He further shows how true love in the heart of the believer is enacted by the grace that is shown from Mary and her Son:

> So, good Son, I ask you through the love you have for your mother, that as she truly loves you and you her you will grant that I may truly love her. Good mother, I ask you by the love you have for your Son, that, as he truly loves you and you him, you will grant that I may love him truly. For see, I am asking what it is indeed your will to do, for why does he not act as my sins deserve when it is in his power.[438]

We see here how deeply Anselm is aware of the distance which exists between him and God, a chasm of his inability to love God which cannot be bridged but by the intercession of the saints.

Beyond the Holy Spirit as the love shared between the Father and Son, and between creature and Creator, Anselm speaks of the person of the Holy Spirit bringing about empowered actions. In the *Meditations* particularly, a picture emerges of the Holy Spirit as enabler in the life of the believer. The believer is not only enabled to love God by the very love which the Father shares with the Son, he or she is empowered by the Holy Spirit, through the gift of grace and redemption which comes from Christ, to activities of the heart and mind honor God. Without the work of the Holy Spirit this honor

---

[437] "Kind Lord and Lady, do not make it difficult to pray to you, but give my soul your love, which not unjustly it asks and you justly expect it to ask, lest I be ungrateful for your good gifts because of that which in justice it shudders at you not unjustly punish." Ibid, 125.

[438] Ibid, 126.

could not be shown because of sin. He indicates freedom from sin is possible only by the work of Christ for redemption and the work of the Holy Spirit for He "didst loose me from my original bonds by the waters of holy baptism and the Holy Spirit's renovation."[439] The Holy Spirit enables his speech, allowing him to exhort others and bring them to the proper place of fear and love of God: "Put, I pray Thee, a word of comfort, of edification, of exhortation, into my mouth by the Holy Spirit."[440] The Holy Spirit brings the penitent to a place where they are aware of their sins and grieve for them: "Open the eyes of my heart by the Holy Spirit, that I may see and bewail my sins."[441] Finally, the Holy Spirit brings the believer into a lifestyle of doing God's will, in all aspects of life. Anselm prays to the Lord: "Do Thou here and ever, now and always, dispose the days of my life in the order of Thy good pleasure, and by Thy Holy Spirit direct my heart, my tongue, and my actions by Thy mercy in accordance to Thy will."[442] Thus the Holy Spirit empowers the believer to act out the will of God in this life, affecting their speech patterns, their desires, and the very activities of daily life to be in keeping with how God desires us to live.

We have noted in this section how Anselm is keenly aware of the personal nature of the Holy Spirit, balanced with the divinity of this person who shares co-equally with the nature of the triune Godhead. It is through the empowerment of the Holy Spirt the believer is able to live the life God requires. It

---

[439] Eighteenth Meditation: Thanksgiving for the benefits of divine mercy, and prayer for the divine assistance. All quotations in this section are from M.R., trans. *St. Anselm of Canterbury: Book of Meditations and Prayers*. (London: Burns and Gates, 1872). Republished as *St. Anselm of Canterbury: Book of Meditations and Prayers. Translated from the Latin by M.R. with a Preface by Henry Edward Cardinal Manning*. Paul A Boer, Sr., ed. Veritas Splendor Publications, 2013.

[440] Ibid.

[441] Ibid.

[442] Ibid.

is by the work of Christ that the debt of honor is paid, and it is by the work of the Holy Spirit that the debt of love is paid. Finally it is by the enabling of the Holy Spirit in the mind that God is able to reveal Himself in an understandable way. Only through the efforts of the Holy Spirit is faith in its seeking rewarded with understanding.

Bernard and the Holy Spirit as Revelation

As we have seen, Bernard's life work was his *Commentary of the Song of Songs*, and just as his Christology may therein be seen, so may his pneumatology. Ever drawing upon the imagery of the poem, while steering clear of its *eros* for the sake of his fellow monks, Bernard invokes the picture of a kiss shared by lovers. This reading becomes very difficult in that the imagery is laden with other unintended context and for todays' reader the picture becomes confused. Bernard uses the relationship in the poem between Bride and Groom as analogous of the love between God and His created beings, but he also uses the poem to speak to a Trinitarian allegory where the Bridegroom is the Father, the Bride is Christ, and the kiss shared between them is the Holy Spirit.[443] In reading this we must not be distracted by impure mental imagery, for Bernard intends this as a representation of the purest love that can exist, the love between the Father and the Son. It is better to envision the pure love, which is God's very nature, expressed analogously in these persons, than to consider the kiss to be an action exchanged between persons. Bernard does not see this an indicating anything more than the purest expression of love in Trinitarian relationship. He states: "If, as is properly understood, the

---

[443] Of this Cristiani states: "Following Origen, Bernard saw the Song of Songs as an epithalamium, or collection of nuptial songs. It was a kind of ancient drama, involving two choirs surrounding the bridegroom and bride, one choir being the bridegroom's friends and the other the bride's." Leon Cristiani, *St. Bernard of Clairvaux* (Boston, MA: The Daughters of St. Paul, 1977), 60.

Father is he who kisses, the Son he who is kissed, then it cannot be wrong to see in the kiss the Holy Spirit, for he is the imperturbable peace of the Father and the Son, their unshakeable bond, their undivided love, their indivisible unity."[444]

Christ in turn passes on the love shared between Himself and the Father to His church. Bernard uses the reference from the Gospel of John where Christ after his resurrection breathes upon the disciples and says: "Receive the Holy Spirit." Bernard sees this breathing upon the disciples as a form of a kiss and representing the impartation of the purest love in the person of the Holy Spirit which the believer can now receive personally. The breathing is not the key aspect of the narrative, but rather the impartation of "the invisible Spirit, who is bestowed in that breath of the Lord that he is understood to proceed from him equally as from the Father, truly the kiss that is common both to him who kisses and to him who is kissed."[445] In this way, the believer receives from Christ the gift of being able to love in the manner intended in creation, in that the person of the Holy Spirit resides within him or her. Cristiani tells us: "Bernard admitted the love of Jesus Christ, insofar as it is a *sensible* or *affective* love is only a stage leading toward what he called *spiritual* love."[446] The act of grace imparts the pure relationship of love between Father and Son to the church, for "the Holy Spirit indeed is nothing else but the love and the benign goodness of them both."[447] The love of Christ enacts the capability to love God in the believer, simultaneously granting the gift of God's love in the person of the Holy Spirit within the believer

---

[444] *Commentary on the Song of Songs*, Sermon 8, S:2.

[445] Ibid.

[446] Cristiani, *St. Bernard*, 156. Emphases original.

[447] Ibid, S:4.

and affecting the heart in love toward God in a manner that would not be possible from a solely human standpoint.

For Bernard, the Holy Spirit is more than an act and more than an impartation of love. The Holy Spirit is the revelation of God Himself into the world and into the heart and mind of the human person. He states: "It is by giving the Spirit, through whom he reveals, that he shows us himself; he reveals in the gift, his gift is in the revealing. Furthermore, this revelation, which is made through the Holy Spirit, not only conveys the light of knowledge but also lights the fire of love."[448] Thus God gives a gift to his creation, the gift of love but more importantly the gift of His very presence. God is not content to allow general revelation to speak for Himself, or even for the recorded words of Scripture to solely present His message and very nature to the world. God prefers to allow each and every person to experience His presence and so He gifts a relationship of love back to fallen humanity. In this gift He also gives a small part of Himself, revealed personally to each individual believer, and the impartation of His presence ignites love. This beautiful imagery becomes a key aspect of understanding Bernardian theology as seen in the relationship of creature to Creator, Church to Father and Son, and Bride to Groom.

Bernard sees the Holy Spirit as both revelator and instructor, that is to say, revelation by instruction. On a number of occasions, he refers to the words of Scripture as the words of the Holy Spirit himself, speaking wisdom into the life of the believer. "Wisdom," he says, "is a kindly spirit, and easy of access to those who call upon him."[449] Bernard, in retelling the story of Elisha the prophet restoring a dead child to life and in referencing the narrative of Scripture, states: "These

---

[448] Ibid, S:5.
[449] Ibid, Sermon 15: The Name of Jesus, S:1.

deeds were done and described under the Holy Spirit's guidance chiefly for the instruction of people who have succumbed to their own corrupt passions, who have been taught to play the fool by the wisdom of this world."[450] Thus we see for Bernard, Scripture is the words of the Holy Spirit, a physical manifestation of God into the world. Further, the wisdom of the Holy Spirit speaks personally into the life of the believer, contrasting Godly wisdom with that which is tainted by sin. Thus God reveals Himself to the church in the wisdom and instruction from the third member of the Trinity. The richness of God's nature, and that which He is able to reveal of Himself may be seen through the guidance of the Holy Spirit, who wishes for the created order to receive as much of God as is possible. Bernard shows us the depths of revelation which is waiting for the believer:

> O you think we have advanced far enough into a sphere that is holy to God, in unraveling this wonderful mystery, or should we dare follow the Holy Spirit into still more secret places to search for meanings that may yet be attained? For the Holy Spirit searches not only the minds and hearts of men but even the depths of God; so whether it be into our own hearts or into the divine mysteries, I shall be secure in following him wherever he goes.[451]

Bernard calls the Holy Spirit the "heaven-sent Director, who can teach us all things", and goes on to show the Holy Spirit can help the believer to distinguish between true wisdom and the seeming-wisdom of the world.[452] Human beings must rely on the person of the Holy Spirit to "observe the distinction

---

[450] Ibid, Sermon 16: Meaning of the Number '7' and the Qualities of True Confession, S:1.

[451] Ibid, Sermon 17: On the Ways of the Holy Spirit and the Envy of the Devil.

[452] Ibid.

between what is clear and what is doubtful" and "must hope for the direction of the Spirit, for even assiduous efforts on our part may be altogether insufficient."[453] It is this instruction from the Holy Spirit which reveals God's nature as His wisdom in the life of the believer.

Bernard sees the working of the Spirit as operating in two distinct manners, what he calls infusion and effusion. Infusion is the process by which the Holy Spirt is poured into the life of the believer, infusing her with the love which is God's very nature. Human beings are unable to love in the manner they were intended and cannot overcome the insult to God which has resulted from sin. Infusion "inwardly strengthens the virtues that lead us to salvation."[454] The reason of the fallen creature, acting on its own, is unable to choose to turn to God and the soul of the creature is unable to love God with the purity and passion which was intended in creation. Thus the action of the Holy Spirit is required in the mind and heart of the believer, to turn them to right choosing and enable love in their lives. This requires the act of infusion by which the Holy Spirit by his very presence brings the creature to an ability to love and choose right.

Effusion is that action by which "he outwardly endows us with serviceable gifts."[455] This is just as important for Bernard in that humankind is created and called to love God, an ability which we have seen is enabled only by the presence of God the Holy Spirit within the individual. Simultaneously, human beings are called to love each other and to perform considerate acts of service. Effusion is dependent on infusion, for without the overwhelming power and presence of the Holy Spirit in the life of the believer, they are unable

---

[453] Ibid.

[454] Sermon 18: The Two Operations of the Holy Spirit.

[455] Ibid.

to allow that presence to be manifest to others in good deeds.[456] A saturation must take place, whereby the believer is so filled with the love of God from the Holy Spirit that an overflow takes place and becomes visible acts of service for fellow human beings. Thus the love of God so overwhelms the heart of the believer that if flows out from them as love for fellow. Bernard shows this in saying: "If, before you are totally permeated by the infusion of the Holy Spirit, you rashly proceed to pour out yourself upon others...you deprive yourself of the life and salvation which you impart to another."[457] Further this deprivation results from "lacking right intention and inspired by self" and the end result is "you become infected with the poison of worldly ambition that swells into a deadly ulcer of decay and destroys you."[458]

This is a warning to those who, wishing to do good deeds, lack the infusion of the Holy Spirit which results in an effusion of grace and love toward others. Bernard shows that the believer should consider their life more like a reservoir than a canal, for a canal merely transports that with which it is filled. But a reservoir cannot pass on its water unless it is so filled as to be overflowing. This overflowing with the love of God results in proper love for others, not merely a vain attempt at service to receive self-glory. Bernard concludes this analogy by saying: "You too must learn to await this fullness before pouring out your gifts, do not try to be more generous than God."[459] Sommerfeldt writes: "Love is the perfection of the will. But the perfection of the will involves the perfection of the affective soul, the feelings, in carnal love just as it brings to fruition the rational faculty's perfection, humility....Love fulfills the lover; the fulfillment is the gift of

---

[456] Cristiani, *St. Bernard*, 47.

[457] Sermon 18: The Two Operations of the Holy Spirit.

[458] Ibid.

[459] Ibid.

God, the indwelling of the Holy Spirit."[460] We see then a deeply personal relationship between the believer and the Holy Spirit. God's revelation within the heart of the believer is love itself, is affective love back toward God, and is due to an intimacy between the human person and God Himself within.

It must be remembered that a person is only enabled to love God and others by the infusion of grace and the revelation of God Himself through the person of the Holy Spirit. Bernard is often optimistic about the condition of humanity because God in His perfection created beings with the capacity to love. Sommerfeldt elucidates this in saying: "Bernard insists that people's naturally good inclinations, themselves gifts of God, are complemented and fulfilled by grace, God's further gifts. Grace perfects nature in the production of the empathy which flows from humility and leads to love."[461] However that optimism is counterbalanced by an Augustinian warning against the sin of pride. [462] Because God has a right to our love, and sin is failing to return love to God, failing to love is also the sin of seeing oneself as a god. This sin of pride can only be overcome by another gift from God, and that is His kiss. In this way we return to the observations made at the beginning of this section, where for Bernard the Holy Spirit is not merely represented in the kiss between Father and Son, but between God and believer as well.

---

[460] John Sommerfeldt, *The Spiritual Teachings of Bernard of Clairvaux* (Kalamazoo, MI: Cistercian Publications, 1991), 100.

[461] Ibid, 90.

[462] Evans presents an excellent overview of Bernard's twelve steps of humility and pride, of which space here precludes further exposition. Her primary concern is that of Bernard's teaching within the monastic community of which he was both a part and the head, and his concern for faithful following of the Benedictine Rule. G. R. Evans, *Bernard of Clairvaux* (New York: Oxford University Press, 2000), 39ff.

Bernard clarifies and strengthens this comparison by demonstrating the difference between the kiss shared by the Father and Son in purest love, and the kiss returned by the penitent to his lord. The Master holds the right to our love, and the Holy Spirit enables us to return that love which is owed, thereby bridging the gulf of sin. He uses the analogy of a feudal relationship (which in turn is mirrored in church authority as well) where the one who owes the master is first at his feet. Then when his first gift of penitence, kissing the feet, is received by the lord, the penitent rises a small amount in order to place a kiss upon the ring of the master. Bernard insists the believer is not to view this rising up as an act of pride, for it is only following the humility of the kiss on the feet of the master that the kiss on the hand is received at all. Bernard equates pride to kissing one's own hand saying: "For if you glory in yourself rather than in the Lord, it is your own hand that you kiss, not his, which, according to the words of Job, is the greatest evil and a denial of God."[463] Sommerfeldt again comments: "Anyone who would be God, who sees oneself as the master of one's world, deceives oneself: he or she is not God. When one acts on this misinformation one chooses incorrectly: one does not truly love."[464] The creature is created to love, the believer is required to love, and the Holy Spirit enables love through humility.

Finally for Bernard the mystic, this love returned to the Father reaches its highest expression in mystical union. When the believer in abject humility receives the enabling action of the Holy Spirit to return the love of God to their lord and master, the desire of the believer is for nothing other than that moment. The penitent may become enraptured by love for God, united to God the Father, Son, and Holy Spirit

---

[463] *Commentary on the Song of Songs*, Sermon 4: The Kiss of the Lord's feet, Hands, and Mouth.

[464] Sommerfeldt, *Spiritual Teachings*, 96.

in intimate union. Gilson elaborates: "In short, the love of God, when brought to this degree of intensity, has something of the character of heavenly beatitude, inasmuch as it is an end in itself, the possession of which dispenses with all the rest because it includes it."[465] In his introduction to the *Commentary on the Song of Songs*, Bernard references the purpose of the Song of Songs as well as the purpose of God in creating: "We must conclude then it was a special divine impulse that inspired these songs of his that now celebrate the praises of Christ and his Church, the gift of holy love, the sacrament of endless union with God."[466]

This for Bernard is the whole purpose of creation, of the existence humankind, of the Incarnation and the special revelation of God to human beings. It is his underlying theme throughout his works and must be understood as Bernard's primary focus. By describing from the outset a mystical union with God as a sacrament, Bernard indicates what he feels to be the very purpose of humanity; that is, to love God and in so doing to return to one's master the love to which He has a right. This action, coupled with humility, enacted in the life of the believer by the Incarnation, and enabled by the person of the Holy Spirit, returns the believer to the position for which they were created. This is reminiscent of the *rectitudo* of Anselm whereby the flawed creature is returned to their rightful state, a state of intimacy with God. Union with God must be the highest goal and purpose of any human being, attainable yet far off for most of us.

---

[465] Etienne Gilson, *The Mystical Theology of Saint Bernard*, trans. A.H.C. Downes (London: Sheed and Ward, 1955), 111.

[466] *Commentary on the Song of Songs*, Sermon 1: On the Title of the Book, S:8.

The Holy Spirit as Love and Dilection

Thomas Aquinas begins his discussion of the Holy Spirit in the *Summa Theologiae* by building upon common themes of his day, themes which we have seen laid out first by Bernard. He immediately introduces the Holy Spirt as Person, as the Love of God, as the impulse of love from the creature back to the Creator, and as proceeding from the Father and the Son. He does not spend much time in analyzing these themes because by the 13th century these Trinitarian considerations were already widely accepted within not only Church circles but within theological circles of the universities as well.[467] What Aquinas does is repackage the arguments made in favor of the Holy Spirit representing these aspects of divinity and wraps them up neatly and logically as is his way. He shows that Spirit speaks to God's *otherness*, "because by 'spirit' the immateriality of the divine substance is signified."[468] Then he shows that the Spirit cannot proceed only from the Father as that would imply that Spirit and Son are merely two separate relations to the Father and could therefore be considered the same person. Though they share the same divine essence, they must be distinguished from each other, and the procession of the Holy Spirit from the Father *and from the Son* establishes this differentiation. Where Anselm prepared an entire work to speak to this argumentation and to prepare for the Council of Bari, Aquinas covers the arguments for the procession of the Holy Spirit from the Son and the Father in a matter of a few pages,

---

[467] Smith lays out how Thomas goes beyond the foundation laid by Augustine, and draws upon advancements made in the Latin terminology used in philosophical discussion (particularly Boethius), to show that God not only can but must exist in three Persons, each of whom shares co-equally in the divine essence.
Timothy Smith, *Thomas Aquinas' Trinitarian Theology* (Washington, D.C.: Catholic University of America Press, 2003), 96-97.

[468] *ST*, I.36.2.

concluding with not only a logical procession but in fact a necessary one. In this manner he speaks to a concern of doctrine within the Church which had been a point of contention for centuries. He does so in a way which not only does not add more distance between Eastern and Western Churches, but rather flatly leaves any disparate opinion without a logical leg to stand upon.

Aquinas, in his development of the Holy Spirit in the *Summa Theologiae*, further reveals the Holy Spirit is best seen as divine revelation. He indicates that just as *Word* is a proper name of the Son and reveals God to the intellect, so *Love* is a proper name for the Spirit and reveals God to the will. The human will responds to God's self-revelation, through the gift of the Holy Spirit, with love and dilection (Latin: *dilectio*).[469] In this section he embarks upon a difficult development of Latin grammar and tells the reader that he does not prefer these two terms but cannot come up with any alternate terminology which accurately describes this relationship. By using the words *love* and *dilection* he establishes love first as an action from the Creator to the creature and when the creature has been acted upon by God's love through the presence of the Holy Spirit, he or she returns this love by choice, an action which he refers to as dilection. Thus God is the source of love, and human beings are capable of love once it has been both acted upon them and enacted within them by the person of the Holy Spirit. Human beings are only capable of returning God's love because He loved them first. God's love is the agency of love returned by the creature.

Not only is the Holy Spirit the revelation of God in the human person and the agent of love returned to the Father from the creature, He is also the love which is returned to the Father by the Son. The Holy Spirit shares the divine essence and

---

[469] *ST*, I.37.1.

also represents, not as medium but as person, the love shared between the members of the Godhead. Thomas uses this discussion to establish first the Holy Spirit proceeds not just from the Father but from the Father and Son, equally as their love for each other. Additionally, because of this procession, the Holy Spirit is God in the world who inspires love returned to the Father and the Son by the creature.

> But when the term Love is taken in a notional sense it means nothing else than 'to spirate love'; just as to speak is to produce a word, and to flower is to produce flowers. As therefore we say that a tree flowers by its flower, so do we say that the Father, by the Word or the Son, speaks Himself, and His creatures; and that the Father and the Son love each other and us, by the Holy Ghost, or by Love proceeding.[470]

Where this is important to the current discussion is that for Aquinas love in the human person is produced only by the love which God Himself gives to us by the presence of the Holy Spirit. It is only because God is present with each of us who believe that the believer is capable of returning God's love. Aquinas shows God is made *understandable* by the giving of Wisdom to the creature, Wisdom who is seen as a Person in the Incarnation of the Son. Further, God is made *relatable* by Love, who is also a Person given to humanity to enable human beings to return to the relationship with God for which they were made.

So the Holy Spirit has been gifted to humanity as God's self-revelation in a personal and immanently relatable way. The Holy Spirit brings other gifts as He enacts God's love within the life of the believer. The first gifts He brings are the moral virtues: temperance, prudence, justice, and courage.

---

[470] *ST*, I.37.2.

Dauphinais and Levering show so beautifully how these virtues are infused within the believer as gifts from God through the Holy Spirit, but the believer not forced to live a life evidenced by the infused virtues. Rather the Holy Spirit enables a development of these infused virtues, lived out, if the believer chooses to act upon what is enacted within them. They state:

> Insofar as theses virtues are gifts from God, they are called *infused* moral virtues; insofar as they are learned by upbringing and practice, they are called *acquired* moral virtues. Within the life of grace, the infused moral virtues allow the person to love God and to love neighbor, and display the reality that grace leaves no aspect of our lives untransformed. The acquired moral virtues, however, are not irrelevant. They allow the person with the infused moral virtues to act with greater ease and alacrity, or readiness. The moral virtues as a whole can be viewed as those good habits that allow us to act justly with ourselves, with those near to us, and with our wider society.[471]

So the Holy Spirit is a gift from God, but as God Himself, is gifted by Himself, just as Christ chose to give Himself freely as the Atonement for sin. The gifts of the Holy Spirit activate the infused moral virtues and turn them toward God, while simultaneously granting the acquired moral virtues which through grace enable the life of love. Additionally for Aquinas love in the believer *is* the image of God, the potential of the *imago dei.* If God is love, and the Holy Spirit is God, the presence of the Holy Spirit renews the love that was lost

---

[471] Michael Dauphinais and Matthew Levering, *Knowing the Love of Christ* (Notre Dame: University of Notre Dame Press, 2002), 51.

through sin.[472] Aquinas adds a unique distinction here in that not only is the Holy Spirit self-gifted, but He gives himself to human persons out of the divine eternity, into a moment in time.[473] This immanent God calling His creatures back into union with Himself and enacting that union through love which would be impossible for the creature to give without the presence of God Himself in the life of the believer. It is accommodation for the divine eternal essence to be limited by time as is the created order.

The Holy Spirit as Wisdom and Restoration

The further gift given by the Holy Spirit is the ability to restore the relationship of human beings to the Father. Just as we saw the Holy Spirit brings the gifts of the moral virtues which are both infused within the believer and acquired when acted upon, so the Holy Spirit brings the gifts of the theological virtues of faith, hope, and love. Thomas points out these virtues are enacted within the human person in accordance with the nature of God: "Our faith is ruled according to Divine truth; charity, according to His goodness; hope, according to the immensity of His omnipotence and loving kindness."[474] Dauphinais and Levering again tell us: "The moral and the theological virtues give us the power to be in relationship to God."[475] The creature can only relate to God to the extent that creature becomes like God. Sin is in opposition to the character and nature of the divine essence;

---

[472] Davies: "For him [Aquinas], charity in people is the image of what the Holy Spirit is. Indeed it is the presence of the Holy Spirit because it is caused by the Holy Spirit. 'God's love has been poured into our hearts through the Holy Spirit which has been given to us', says St. Paul [Rom 5.5]. Aquinas takes this to mean that the Christian virtue of charity is the effect in us of the Holy Spirit, who thereby produces in us what love is in God." Brian Davies, *The Thought of Thomas Aquinas* (Oxford: Clarendon Press, 1992), 289. *ST*, II-II.23.2.

[473] *ST*, I.38.1.

[474] *ST*, I-II.64.4.

[475] Dauphinais and Levering, *Knowing*, 51.

therefore nothing could be more unlike God than sin. Because all human beings are born tainted by original sin, we can never be like God enough to relate to Him. This then is the twofold purpose of God's immanence to the world: first to establish a means to be returned into right standing through the Incarnation and Atonement, and second to enact a way to live like God in this world through the infusion of grace and the gifts of the Holy Spirit.

Not only is the Holy Spirit seen as Love - love as a person, love from the Father, and love returned by the creature - the Holy Spirit in Aquinas is also Wisdom personified. God in His transcendence cannot be known by humankind except that He reveal Himself in a knowable way. For God to be understood even in part He must impart some knowledge and wisdom to the creature.[476] Anselm Min lays out the purpose of Thomas' theology which is simply knowing God; this is the highest goal and task of the human person. He states: "Theology therefore, is wisdom in the highest sense, above all human wisdom including metaphysics. Although a knowledge acquired through study, not infused as one of the gifts of the Holy Spirit, it is nonetheless knowledge of what is the highest, most universal, and most ultimate in all human experience."[477] Holding this knowledge which is gained by human learning and experience in contradistinction to those gifts which are given by the Holy Spirit is important because for Aquinas this is the choice which the human person must make. The creature must be participant, not in the act of grace or in infusion of the moral virtues, but in striving to

---

[476] Timothy Smith states: "The incomprehensibility of God then remains a fundamental part of Thomas' theology. The insurmountable inadequacy of human knowing with respect to the essence of God is due to the infinity of God and the finitude of our minds." It is only as God reveals Himself and as the Holy Spirit imparts wisdom that God becomes knowable at all. Smith, *Trinitarian Theology*, 78.

[477] Anselm Min, *Paths to the Triune God* (Notre Dame: University of Notre Dame Press, 2005), 137. Also *SCG* 3.37ff.

the highest goal which is to know God. Gilson here tells us: "The gift of wisdom, then, does not add a superior reason to the natural superior reason, but it causes reason, in its investigation of the divine, to feel at it were at home therein, instinctively sensing what is true, long before grasping its demonstration."[478] Divine wisdom builds upon the natural reason in cooperation with the concerted effort on the part of the believer to know God. Divine Wisdom is God immanently revealed to the believer in Word and in Love, driving the reason to its ultimate goal, knowledge and communion with God. Min goes on to show: "As *human* wisdom, however, theology is possible only by sharing in the 'light' of divine wisdom."[479] This light is the person of the Holy Spirit, the third member of the Godhead, revealing God to human beings and representing His presence in the world.

Just as in love, the Son and the Spirit cooperate in the believer to bring about wisdom. God cannot be loved by fractured humanity except He reveals Himself as Word, the relatable means God uses to communicate Himself to the creature. Further the word must be established in the believer and nurtured by the Holy Spirit to enact love. Legge expresses this in saying: "Just as the perfect Word of the Father breathes forth the Holy Spirit (the Father and his Word spirate the Holy Spirit) so also the sending of the Word to the soul breaks forth into the love in which there is a mission of the Holy Spirit."[480] In like manner, the Son and Spirit work together to bring about wisdom in the life of the believer. Legge adds: "[I]n the gifts of wisdom and charity, it is by exemplar causality that the soul is assimilated to a likeness of the divine persons: according to their eternal

---

[478] Etienne Gilson, *Thomism: The Philosophy of Thomas Aquinas*, 6th ed., trans. Armand Maurer (Toronto: Pontifical Institute of Medieval Studies, 2002), 395.

[479] Ibid.

[480] Dominic Legge, *The Trinitarian Christology of St. Thomas Aquinas* (Oxford: Oxford University Press, 2017), 31.

processions by way of knowledge and love, the Son and the Holy Spirit are the models to which we are conformed by those gifts."[481] This conforming to the nature of the Father is the intended goal He had in creation, it is also unattainable in this earthly life. However Thomas shows that by the infusion of the Holy Spirt as God and Person, and by His gifts which enable the virtues, a process is begun in the life of the believer which when it reaches its final end results in the human person becoming as like God as possible. Dauphinais and Levering refer to this process as "divinization" and show it is the culmination of the revelation of God.[482] They add: "But how do we know what God has revealed? God is not only the content of faith, but also the giver of faith. God Himself inspires us to assent to the fullness of truth 'as proposed in the Scriptures, according to the teaching of the Church which has the right understanding of them'".[483] Only as God reveals Himself as Word and Wisdom, and as the virtues are infused by the presence of the Holy Spirit can the human person begin this process of living out God's nature. This begins with faith which is seeded by God, planted in the revealed Word of God, watered by the Wisdom of God, and nurtured by the love which is shared between creature and Creator.[484]

So we see the Holy Spirit is God immanently revealing Himself, giving Himself into the world to restore fallen humanity to its rightful relationship with God. The Son and the Spirit collaborate to instill human reason with the

---

[481] Ibid.

[482] Dauphinais and Levering, *Knowing*, 53-54.

[483] Ibid. Quoting *ST*, II-II.5.3.

[484] O'Meara states this well: "The next life will not be an eternity of distractions but an unimaginable communion with Wisdom and Love, a life which never tires or bores. God not only gives happiness but is the reward: The Trinity is the 'light of glory'....Grace's destiny is always silently inviting and blessing human life." Thomas O'Meara, *Thomas Aquinas: Theologian* (Notre Dame: University of Notre Dame Press, 1997), 150.

knowledge of God and to enact love in the believer which drives their concerted effort toward deeper knowledge. Wisdom and Word are God revealed to human persons, without whom the natural reason would not be capable to bring the human person into a restored state of communion. This communion is attainable in its perfection only in the life to come, although the Son and the Spirit immanently bridge the gap to God's transcendence in the mind and heart of the believer. O'Meara tells of this future, this perfect state to which God has called us:

> Heaven's vison of God brings gifts which enable human beings to transcend the limitations of matter, and to fulfill on a higher plane individual personality. Love heightens as it expands toward vast communities of men and women. What was a sluggish and meager interest in God and religion on earth becomes a high level of wisdom. We see and learn endlessly, as the divine vision eternally inspires and amazes.[485]

This is the intended goal for the human creature, the state which God desired us to attain from the beginning. The corruption of the human reason and emotions left us unable to achieve that state for which we were created, and God in His mercy and Wisdom enacted a way through the giving of Himself to begin restoration of the *imago dei*.

---

[485] Ibid, 150-151.

CHAPTER SEVEN:
IMMANENCE AND TRANSCENDENCE FOR TODAY'S THEOLOGIANS

As we alluded in the Introduction, not only do the great debates of the church seem to return from time to time, but the writers who speak to those debates for their own moment impart wisdom beyond their individual place in history. Every writer and thinker is an embedded member of their own time, place, and culture, yet because the truths about God are unchanging, even as He Himself is unchanging, the application of those truths may be just as profound one hundred or even one thousand years later. While each of the writers we have explored did not write for our time in history, God has preserved His special revelation in the words of Scripture which, when interpreted and applied to individual points on the timeline, continue to impart His immanence into the present.

The words of Scripture as we have seen thus far were incredibly important for our writers, and must continue to form the foundation of doctrine. We live in complex times and the medievalists could never have foreseen the Reformation, the Renaissance, Humanism, Socialism, World Wars, the Civil Rights movement, or the vast array of incidents and movements which, when piled upon each other, form the basis of modern culture. However they did speak truth, truth for their day which remains truth today, because it is truth about God. This is not to imply that these three writers, or any, should be accepted as dogma without comparison to the foundation of Scripture or to other teachings of the Church. Rather, each imparts a unique viewpoint which tells us more about God, for we have seen that the Reason with which humanity was created is tuned to know more about the Creator. God envisioned a creation which would know Him and love Him and thus created human beings from the beginning. In His almighty power and divine nature, He was always going to be transcendent from the world, but in the Garden, He was immanently relatable, and the First Persons walked and talked with God on a daily basis.

Through original sin, which Augustine tells us was that of pride, the intended intimacy was destroyed, and human persons could never relate to God in the same way. Therefore God chose not to remove human Reason or passion but to direct it back to Himself through His own self-revelation. It is understanding God's transcendence and immanence in this way which allows the theologian of the past and the theologian of today to embark upon a search for deeper knowledge of God and to engage in theology proper. This must be the starting point of theology. For if one does not understand what God has made known about Himself, one cannot go on to understand the purpose of human beings, their place within the created order, the persona and object of the Incarnation, the nature of the Trinity, or the reason for the eventual and inevitable return of the Creator-King to earth.

Earlier we introduced the argument which might state that today's concepts of theology, especially systematic theology, cannot be reverse engineered to apply to a time period in which theologians did not employ either the specific verbiage or concepts. However this must be a fallacy akin to saying one could never understand Luther unless one read German and lived in 15th century Germany. Johannes Zachuber draws us from the past into the present and speaks to the use of terms which although not specifically applied within the time periods we study here, represent universal principles which are today universally applied. He states:

> The binary use of the terms 'transcendence' and 'immanence' is one of the most powerful concepts to have emerged from nineteenth-century debates about religion. It is also one of their most enduring legacies; in fact, the juxtaposition of the two terms, the assumption that they refer to an ontological, epistemic or theological duality, is today taken for granted and conventionally applied to the analysis of religious and other worldviews throughout history and across cultures.[486]

In this way we may apply the concepts embodied in the terms Immanence and Transcendence, which in the 19th century were developed from a systematic understanding of God's nature, back to writings which originated in the 11th, 12th, and 13th centuries. We are able to do so because the terms themselves represent universal concepts, and are simply characteristic of specific language, which was unknown, in their times, to our individual writers.

Augustine, who could never have imagined the great and populous cities of today, reminds us the greatest city is the City of God. He indicates: "But in that city all the citizens shall be immortal, men now for the first time enjoying what the holy angels have never lost. And this shall be accomplished by God, the most almighty Founder of the city."[487] This tells us not only of the purpose for which

---

[486] Johannes Zachuber, "Transcendence and Immanence" in Daniel Whistler, ed. *The Edinburgh Critical History of 19th Century Theology* (Edinburgh: Edinburgh University Press, 2018), 164.

[487] Augustine, *City of God*, Book XXII, ch.1.

humankind was created but the persistent promise which awaits those who endure the harsh difficulties of this life below. While most of the members of our congregations have never read Augustine (and frankly neither have most of our seminarians), God's faithfulness speaks to us from 1500 years in the past. Yet it is only after the reader marches through the origination of sin, understands the fractured nature of humanity, grasps the need and purpose of the Incarnation, and recognizes God's revelation of Himself within the believer that they are then able to understand the greatness of this promise of the City of God. For it is only there that humankind returns to the intimacy with the Father for which they were created and are welcomed as adopted children, underserving of the Father's love. Augustine sets the stage for theologians who would come after and build on the recognition Augustine had of the vast otherness of God coupled with His intimate nearness and self-revelation.

Anselm in his wisdom brings together a synergy of Augustine, the Holy Scriptures, and neoplatonism which was so timely for his generation. Thus Anselm employs similar methodology to that which we here put into practice. He reaches into antiquity to bring truth to light which speaks into his current situation and develops truths which form the bedrock of Church doctrine for nearly a millennium. In his introduction to the *Monologion*, Anselm shows his reader his intense devotion to Augustine, as well as the fact that he is building upon the foundation laid by the great theologian to bring new light and insight to church doctrine.

> In the course of frequent rereadings of this treatise I have been unable to find anything which is inconsistent with the writing of the Catholic Fathers, and in particular with those of the Blessed Augustine. If, then, someone

thinks that I have said here anything which is either too modern, or which departs from the truth, I would ask them not to denounce me as an arrogant modernizer or a maintainer of falsehood. Rather I ask that they first make a careful reading of the books *On the Trinity* of the aforementioned learned Augustine and then judge my little treatise on the basis of them.[488]

Anselm thus recognizes the danger of approaching historical theology, the dangers to which we have alluded in Chapter Two. This may be termed the "arrogance of the modern" and can be a trap for any historian or theologian. The danger is that one approaches the writers of the Middle Ages, or any bygone age, and assumes that they knew as much about the world as we do now. We can easily forget they existed in a time that was quite different from our own, before the realization was made the world was round, for instance, or the sun the center of the solar system. Where that affects one's view of the ancients then is one can discount their concerns, or write off their impact both their society and to our own owing to the fact that they simply were not as knowledgeable.

Anselm of course recognizes his writings could be critiqued in the same way and so made every effort to build upon the work of those who came before, particularly the foundational teaching of Augustine who largely was responsible for setting Church doctrine up to the time of the scholastics. In the same way we can and must value the contribution of those whom we here study and others upon whom we have not had time and space to comment. Anselm shows today's reader the value of a heart and mind attuned to God. Where one may critique his argument which far later came to be called

---

[488] *Mono*, Prologue.

the ontological proof for God's existence, today's theologian must realize the value of Anselm's focus on *fides quarens intellectum,* faith seeking understanding.[489] To begin from a position of belief enables a theologian to grasp what may be known about God, while employing rational thought and human reason to seek to know more. It is when we approach Holy Scripture and the words of those who have come before from a position not dissimilar to that of the Apostle Thomas in the book of John, who could not believe what he could not know both existentially and ontologically, that we fail to gain knowledge which builds our faith. Knowledge can certainly be an end in itself, but understanding coupled with and founded upon belief allows one to know God Himself, not just information about Him.

Anselm further shows us that not just the mind must be engaged in gaining knowledge about God. For God wants our hearts too, and desires the intimacy and connection for which He created humankind in the first place. Here we see from Anselm's prayers and meditations a person whose heart and mind were focused on knowing God, and the reward is communion with the divine, imperfectly in this life and perfectly in the one to come.[490] The mind is for the present life and understanding is of value while on this earth, but when eternity is reached, the believer is rewarded with

---

[489] Of course, Aquinas nearly 200 years later takes such a liberty, demonstrating the failure of Anselm in this case to adhere to the laws of logic. Thomas by that time had the advantage of exposure to The Philosopher.

[490] "But, He who bestows on His own such great blessings in the present, what does He reserve for them in the future?...If thy life is a burden to thee, the world a weariness, and the flesh a grief, then surely death is thy desire; death that removes this burdensome yoke, and ends fatigue, and takes away the body with its pain. This one event, I tell thee, transcends all the delights, all the honours, and all the riches of the world; if only by reason of a cloudless conscience, a faith not to be shaken, and a certain hope, that art not afraid to die."
Seventeenth Meditation: Of Future Benefits from God.

perfect knowledge, unclouded by original sin.[491] At that time, the heart which chose to believe in this life is also rewarded with perfect communion with God, and humankind is returned to that state for which they were created. Theology can be a struggle, as any doctoral student can sympathize. Human beings are simply not capable of knowing God fully, and Anselm speaks with clarity to His transcendence in this way. Yet God desires to be known to the extent that we can, and provides a series of means which speak to His nature in a comprehensible way. Thus the value of reading Anselm is to see that when applied to theology proper, the *Doctor Magnificus* shows the one willing to explore his works the co-equal aspects of God's otherness and self-revelation. This theologian is both rewarded with Anselm's enlightening the mind and emotions to deeper knowledge of God and is simultaneously reminded to keep the two aspects of God's nature in balanced juxtaposition.

Bernard likewise spoke both into his own time and continues to speak across the centuries. He is far more challenging to approach than is Anselm and McGuire calls him "The Difficult Saint".[492] Bernard can be difficult in that he was accustomed to speaking to the highest levels of church and civil authority in his day, and his tone can reflect a certain denigration as a result. Once the reader gets beyond a sense of disparagement however, one sees Bernard calling his listeners and readers to the joy of loving God in the manner for which we were intended. Bernard portrays a certain feudal conception of the duty we have in returning to God the love which is His by right and that is where the reader must understand Bernard to be speaking into his own place in history. The value of love is right relationship however and

---

[491] Anselm many times in *Cur Deus Homo* speaks to the future of humankind with implicit reference to Augustine, referring to heaven as a city.

[492] Brian McGuire, *The Difficult Saint* (Kalamazoo, MI: Cistercian, 1991).

this is a universal truth which may be gleaned from the *Mellifluous Doctor*. Bernard also indicates as did Anselm, that the mind and heart must be simultaneously concerted in their effort of knowing God which culminates in intimacy. He writes: "Only the mind disciplined by persevering study, only the man whose efforts have borne fruit under God's inspiration, the man whose years, as it were, make him ripe for marriage, years measured not in time but in merits – only he is truly prepared for nuptial union with the divine partner."[493]

When we read his *Sermons* and *Commentary on the Song of Songs*, we are reminded that Bernard speaks of the distance which exists between creature and Creator by virtue of original sin. Only when the gulf is bridged by the love of God and the sacrifice of the Savior can communion be attained. Further only when the Holy Spirit enables love in the believer can right standing by attained before God who deserves our return of love to Him. This understanding of God's great distance from the world and from the human person is coupled in Bernard with a balanced view toward God's self-revelation, without which knowledge of God and union with God would be impossible. Only God's self-revelation in the grace brought about by the Incarnation coupled with the spirating work of the third person of the Trinity, God Himself revealed in the Holy Spirt given to the believer, enables the believer to come to Him. The rational person must chose to accept grace, and thereby cooperate with grace for salvation, but this is the extent of the effort which can be made by any person. Further this consent of the reason to grace, though it is an act of the will, is an act of accepting freedom.[494] Freedom to accept grace and turn to God results in

---

[493] *Commentary on the Song of Songs*, Sermon 1: On the Title of the Book, S:12.

[494] *On Grace and Free Will*, Chapter 1: That to the merit of a good work is needed, together with the grace of God, the consent of the free will.

relationship and intimacy, the like of which can only be compared to the closeness of marriage.

Bernard shows how in the intimacy of this relationship, humankind is restored to their rightful place. That this takes an act of the Divine will is certain, coupled with a spirated act of the human will. When these two take place, God's transcendence is bridged by His immanence, becoming really real to the human believer. As Anselm showed, the mind may work to attain knowledge of God, but only the heart can be rewarded with true communion. For Bernard, this is the greatest way in which he could show the twin attributes of God's immanence and transcendence, for God in His wisdom imparts some of His wisdom to His creation and inspires them to find Him. While it is true God exists on a wholly other plane and in His omniscience knows far beyond the limited scope of human beings, simultaneously, the Son is personified Wisdom and as such is revelation, wisdom which is revealed and attainable by the human person. This cannot be through sheer exercise of the mind, but in embracing Wisdom the believer embraces God's revelation of Himself. By God's revelation of Himself in Wisdom personified and in the words of Holy Scripture, the human person may be filled with true wisdom which:

> Causes the fear of God and the observance of His commandments to be preferred to all human pursuits and worldly desires. And rightly so, for the former is the beginning of wisdom, the latter its culmination, for there is no true and consummate wisdom other than the avoidance of evil and the doing of good, no one can successfully shun evil without the fear

of God, and no work is good without the observance of the commandments.[495]

This Bernard teaches as the steps in this life to attain the closest one can to communion with God. The rest and the best will have to wait till we see Him face to face.

Gerard Verbeke in his treatment of Aquinas' philosophy makes the observation that in a variety of locations, Thomas references humanity as existing on a kind of frontier, situated on the edge between two worlds, the spiritual and the worldly. He states "Therefore man occupies an intermediate position with the whole of reality: he does not belong entirely to the superior domain, the intelligible, nor to the inferior level, the sensible. Both spheres of reality are combined in the concrete unity of his being and are no longer separated from each other as, for example, two adjacent geographical areas."[496] The value for understanding this position is, for the theologian, just as applicable as for the philosopher. For human beings, whom God created with purpose, are given the ability to reason and to emote, and in some limited way to know God because of those faculties. God has revealed Himself in approachable ways and calls human beings to live in these two worlds. We are tied to the physical yet seek the spiritual. The unique aspect of relating to God is that the closer we get to God, the further we are withdrawn from those more tangible things we can touch in this world.

Scott Hahn interacts with this concept, not in a purely Thomist manner but in a catholic way when he references Christians using the analogy of whales. Whales are air

---

[495] *Commentary on the Song of Songs*, Sermon 1: On the Title of the Book.

[496] Gerard Verbeke, "Man as Frontier According to Aquinas" in Gerard Verbeke, ed. *Aquinas and the Problems of his Time* (The Hague: Leuven University Press, 1976), 195.

breathing creatures that live in the water, thus for the majority of their life they are surrounded by the water domain in which they live, feed, breed, and interact with each other. However to breathe they must break the surface of the water to fill their lungs with oxygen and thereby enable their return to the world of water in which they exist primarily. In the same way the believer, reflecting this Thomist construct of living on the frontier, may breathe occasionally the breath of heaven and come momentarily into contact with the divine nature, yet must return to this physical world in which they live the majority of the time.[497] This analogy is quite striking when one further considers Thomas' development of the powers of the soul, which include the intellectual powers, the appetitive powers (what we desire), and the power of the will. Of this the *Angelic Doctor* treats particularly on the soul which is the essence of life within the person and is composed of thought life, will, and emotional life. The mind is moved toward God by the impetus of the Holy Spirit who guides and calls the mind of a person into knowledge of God. A person under this influence must move their mind into relation with God as they move their body in relation to the world around them.[498] This is the power of the will to purpose to move oneself toward God. And finally the appetite is drawn toward God through a two-fold process of the higher desires driving the lower. Here Thomas interacts directly with Aristotle, "*The* Philosopher", and morphs his concepts into a theological application whereby the intellectual desires to bring the physical desires on board in seeking to know God.[499]

[497] Scott Hahn, "Scripture and Liturgy" on the Coming Home Network International Youtube channel, https://www.youtube.com/watch?v=e8gGACA_pLE. Accessed 21 Nov 2020.

[498] *ST*, I-I.75.1.

[499] *ST*, I-I.80.2

This discussion in Aquinas is directly related to our overall treatment in this work. For we have seen how God reveals Himself to the world, making Himself immanent where He would otherwise exist solely in a state of total otherness. It is only by this self-revelation that the human mind is capable of conceiving of God and His attributes in part, and the reason drives the desires toward God. When the human person comes into contact with the revealed God in creation and in the Scriptures, when they understand the person of Jesus Christ and His ministry on earth, and when the third person of the Trinity speaks into the mind and heart of the believer, only then are they able to move toward God. This movement is empowered by the revelation of God within the believer in the person and gift of the Holy Spirit, once the human person has cooperated with God in accepting His grace which enables restoration and *rectitudo*.

Finally having explored the depths of medieval treatment of God's co-equal attributes of His transcendence and immanence, and having noted with pleasure the ways in which the doctors of the church have expounded upon these concepts, I conclude with this in mind. The goal of learning about God, the goal of theology, is to know Him and love Him, thereby returning to the state in which and for which God created humankind. This the medievalists exhorted their readers toward, sometimes with philosophy and logic, sometimes with learned discussion, sometimes with the tears and cries of the mystic who travails to know God more deeply. And so I pray, with Anselm, the following prayer for my readers:

> Let not the future terrify you with its barren waste, nor a fear of coming hunger deject your spirits; but let all your trust rest in Him who feeds the birds and clothes the lilies. Let Him be your barn, make Him your treasury, make Him

your purse, Him your riches, Him your joy; let Him alone be all in all to you. And meanwhile let this suffice for the things of the present.[500]

---

[500] *Sixteenth Meditation: Of Present Benefits from God.*

BIBLIOGRAPHY

Translated Primary Sources

Anselm. *The Major Works of St. Anselm.* Translated by Sidney Norton Deane. Chicago: Open Court, 1939.

———. *The Prayers and Meditations of Saint Anselm.* Translated by Benedicta Ward. Harmondsworth, UK: Penguin Books, 1973.

———. *St. Anselm of Canterbury: Book of Meditations and Prayers.* Translated by M.R. London: Burns and Gates, 1872. Republished as *St. Anselm of Canterbury: Book of Meditations and Prayers. Translated from the Latin by M.R. with a Preface by Henry Edward Cardinal Manning.* Paul A Boer, Sr., ed. Veritas Splendor Publications, 2013.

Aquinas, Thomas. *Summa Theologiae.* Translated by multiple translators. London: Blackfriars, 1972.

———. *The Complete Works of Thomas Aquinas.* Translated by multiple translators. Omaha, NE: Catholic Publishing, 2018.

Augustine. *The Complete Works of Saint Augustine.* Translated by multiple translators. Amazon Kindle edition, no publication data, 2013.

Bernard of Clairvaux. *Saint Bernard of Clairvaux: Collection.* Translated by multiple translators. Aeterna Press, 2016. Kindle version.

Davies, Brian and G.R. Evans, eds. *Anselm of Canterbury: the Major Works.* Oxford: Oxford University Press, 1998.

Eadmer. *The Life of St. Anselm.* Translated and edited by R. W. Southern. Oxford; Clarendon Press, 1962.

Plato. *Timaeus.* Translated by Donald J. Zeyl. Indianapolis: Hackett, 2000.

Schaff, Phillip, ed. *The Complete Works of the Church Fathers.* Translated by multiple translators. Kindle edition, Public Domain.

Books

Annas, Julia. *Plato: A Very Short Introduction.* Oxford: Oxford University Press, 2003.

Ayers, Lewis. *Augustine and the Trinity.* Cambridge: Cambridge University Press, 2010.

Barron, Caroline M. and Christopher Harper-Bill, eds. *The Church in Pre-Reformation Society: Essays in Honour of F. R. H. Du Boulay.* Dover, NH: Boydell Press, 1985.

Barron, Robert. *Thomas Aquinas: Spiritual Master.* New York: Crossroad Publishing, 1996.

Brecher, Robert. *Anselm's Argument: The Logic of Divine Existence.* Brookfield, VT: Gower, 1985.

Bright, Pamela, ed. and trans. *Augustine and the Bible.* Notre Dame, IN: University of Notre Dame Press, 1999 (English edition).

Clark, Mary T. *Augustine: Philosopher of Freedom.* New York: Desclee Co., 1958.

————. *Augustine.* London: Geoffrey Chapman, 1994.

Coulton, G.G. (George Gordon), *Ten Medieval Studies, 3rd edition.* Gloucester, MA: Peter Smith, 1967.

Cristiani, Leon. *St. Bernard of Clairvaux.* Boston: Daughters of St. Paul, 1977.

Davies, Brian. *The Thought of Thomas Aquinas.* New York: Oxford University Press, 1992.

————. *Aquinas.* London: Continuum, 2002.

Daniel-Rops, Henri. *Bernard of Clairvaux.* New York: Hawthorne Books, 1964.

Dauphinais, Michael and Matthew Levering. *Knowing the Love of Christ: An Introduction to the Theology of St. Thomas Aquinas.* Notre Dame, IN: University of Notre Dame Press, 2002.

Dauphinais, Michael; Barry David; and Matthew Levering. *Aquinas the Augustinian.* Washington, D.C.: Catholic University of America Press, 2007.

Doolan, Gregory T. *Aquinas on the Divine Ideas as Exemplar Causes.* Washington, D.C.: Catholic University of America Press, 2008.

Elders, Leo J. *The Philosophical Theology of St. Thomas Aquinas.* Leiden, Netherlands: E. J. Brill, 1990.

Emery, Giles and Matthew Levering, eds. *Aristotle in Aquinas' Theology.* Oxford: Oxford University Press, 2015.

Evans, G.R. *Anselm and Talking about God.* Oxford: Oxford University Press, 1978.

————. *Anselm.* Milton, CT: Morehouse-Barlow, 1989.

————. *Bernard of Clairvaux.* New York: Oxford University Press, 2000.

Evans, G. R. ed. *The Medieval Theologians: An Introduction to Theology in the Medieval Period.* Malden, MA: Blackwell, 2001.

————. *The First Christian Theologians.* Malden, MA: Blackwell, 2004.

Fortin, John R., ed. *Saint Anselm - His Origins and Influence.* Lewiston, NY: Edwin Mellen Press, 2001.

Gallagher, Patrick J. and Helen Damico, eds., *Hermeneutics and Medieval Culture.* Albany, NY: State University of New York Press, 1989.

Gaspar, G.E.M. and H. Kihlenberger, eds. *Anselm and Abelard: Investigations and Juxtapositions.* Toronto: Pontifical Institute of Medieval Studies, 2006.

Gaspar, Giles E.M. *Anselm of Canterbury and his Theological Inheritance.* Burlington, VT: Ashgate, 2004.

Gaspar, Giles E. M. and Ian Logan, eds. *Saint Anselm of Canterbury and his Legacy.* Durham: Durham University, 2012.

Gilson, Étienne, *History of Christian Philosophy in the Middle Ages.* New York: Random House, 1955.

————. *The Mystical Theology of St. Bernard.* Translated by A.H.C. Downes. London: Sheed and Ward, 1955.

————. *The Christian Philosophy of Saint Augustine.* Translated by L.EM. Lynch. New York: Random House, 1960.

————. *The Spirit of Thomism.* New York: P.J. Kennedy and Sons, 1964.

————. *Thomism: The Philosophy of Thomas Aquinas, 6th ed.* Translated by Armand Maurer. Toronto: Pontifical Institute of Medieval Studies, 2002.

Grant, Edward. *God and Reason in the Middle Ages.* Cambridge: Cambridge University Press, 2001.

Grenz, Stanley J. and Roger E. Olson. *20th Century Theology: God and the World in a Transitional Age.* Downer's Grove, Ill: Intervarsity Press, 1992.

Grudem, Wayne. *Systematic Theology.* Grand Rapids, MI: Zondervan Publishing House, 1994.

Gurevich, Aron. *Medieval Popular Culture: Problems of Belief and Perception.* Translated by Janos M. Bak and Paula A. Hollingsworth. Cambridge: Cambridge University Press, 1988.

Hall, Christopher A. *Learning Theology with the Church Fathers.* Downer's Grove, Ill: Inter-Varsity, 2002.

Hall, Stuart G. *Doctrine and Practice in the Early Church*. London: SPCK, 1991.

Harrison, Carol. *Rethinking Augustine's Early Christianity: An Argument for Continuity*. Oxford: Oxford University Press, 2006.

Hartshorne, Charles. *Anselm's Discovery: A Re-examination of the Ontological Proof for God's Existence*. LaSalle, Ill: Open Court Publishing, 1965.

Hauser, Alan J. and Duane F. Watson, eds. *A History of Biblical Interpretation: Volume 2, The Medieval through the Reformation Periods*. Grand Rapids: Eerdmans, 2009.

Healy, Nicolas M. *Thomas Aquinas: Theologian of the Christian Life*. Burlington, VT: Ashgate, 2003.

Hogg, David S. *Anselm of Canterbury: The Beauty of Theology*. Burlington, VT: Ashgate, 2004.

Hopkins, Jasper. *A Companion to the Study of St. Anselm*. Minneapolis: University of Minnesota Press, 1972.

Howarth, David. *1066: The Year of the Conquest*. New York: Barnes and Noble, 1977.

Hunt, Ignatius. *The Theology of St. Thomas on the Old Law*. Ottawa: St. Paul's Seminary, 1949.

Keen, Maurice. *The Pelican History of Medieval Europe*. New York: Penguin Books, 1968.

Kelly, J.N.D. *Early Christian Doctrines, 5th ed*. New York: Harper Collins, 1978.

Ku, John Baptist. *God the Father in the Theology of St. Thomas Aquinas*. New York: Peter Lang, 2013.

Lane, Anthony N.S. *Bernard of Clairvaux: Theologian of the Cross*. Collegeville, MN: Liturgical Press, 2013.

Legge, Dominic. *The Trinitarian Christology of St. Thomas Aquinas*. Oxford: Oxford University Press, 2017.

Lienhard, Joseph T.; Earl C. Muller; and Roland J. Teske, eds. *Augustine: Presbyter Factus Sum*. New York: Peter Lang Publishing, 1993.

Livermore, Jeremy. "Augustine". https://apologetics.com.

Lot, Ferdinand. *The End of the Ancient World and the Beginning of the Middle Ages*. Translated by Philip and Mariette Leon. New York: Harper and Brothers, 1961.

Luscombe, D.E. and G.R. Evans, eds. *Anselm: Aosta, Bec and Canterbury*. Sheffield, England: Sheffield Academic Press, 1996.

Macdonald, Paul A, Jr. *Knowledge & the Transcendent: An Inquiry into the Mind's Relationship to God*. Washington, D.C.: Catholic University of America Press, 2009.

Matthews, Gareth B. *Augustine*. Malden, MA: Blackwell, 2005.

McGrath, Alister E. *Iustitia Dei: A History of the Christian Doctrine of Justification*. Cambridge: Cambridge University Press, 2005.

McGuire, Brian. *The Difficult Saint*. Kalamazoo, MI: Cistercian Publications, 1991.

McInerny, Ralph. *A First Glance at St. Thomas Aquinas*. Notre Dame: University of Notre Dame Press, 1990.

McIntyre, John. *St. Anselm and his Critics: A Reinterpretation of the Cur Deus Homo*. Edinburgh: Oliver and Boyd, 1954.

Meconi, David Vincent, SJ. *The One Christ: St. Augustine's Theology of Deification*. Washington, D.C.: Catholic University of America Press, 2013.

Merton, Thomas. *The Ascent to Truth*. San Diego: Harcourt Brace Jovanovich, 1981.

Min, Anselm K. *Paths to the Triune God: An Encounter Between Aquinas and Recent Theologies*. Notre Dame: University of Notre Dame Press, 2005.

Newman, Richard. *Saint Benedict in his Time*. Monmouthshire, Wales: Three Peaks Press, 2013.

O'Loughlin, Thomas. *Early Medieval Exegesis in the Latin West*. Burlington, VY, Ashgate, 2013.

O'Meara, Thomas F. *Thomas Aquinas: Theologian*. Notre Dame: University of Notre Dame Press, 1997.

Pasnau, Robert, ed. *The Cambridge History of Medieval Philosophy*. Cambridge: Cambridge University Press, 2010.

Pasnau, Robert and Christopher Shields. *The Philosophy of Thomas Aquinas*. Boulder, CO: Westview Press, 2004.

Pegis, Anton C. *Basic Writings of Saint Thomas Aquinas*. New York: Random House, 1945.

Pieper, Josef. *Guide to Thomas Aquinas, 3rd ed.* San Francisco: Ignatius Press, 1991. Translated 1962.

Putnam, Rhyne. *In Defense of Doctrine: Evangelicalism, Theology, and Scripture*. Minneapolis: Fortress Press, 2015.

Ramos, Alice. *Dynamic Transcendentals: Truth, Goodness, and Beauty from a Thomistic Perspective*. Washington, D.C: Catholic University of America Press, 2012.

Ratisbonne, Theodore. *St. Bernard of Clairvaux: Oracle of the Twelfth Century*. Rockford, Ill: Tan Books and Publishers, 1991.

Reilly, James P., ed. *The Gilson Lectures on Thomas Aquinas*. Toronto: Pontifical Institute of Medieval Studies, 2008.

Rubin, Miri and Walter Simons, eds. *The Cambridge History of Christianity: Christianity in Western Europe, c. 1100- c. 1500.* Cambridge: Cambridge University Press, 2009.

Shannon, William, H. *Anselm: The Joy of Faith.* New York: Crossroad, 1999

Shriver, George H., ed. *Contemporary Reflections on the Medieval Christian Tradition: Essays in honor of Ray C. Petry.* Durham, NC: Duke University Press, 1974.

Smalley, Beryl. *Studies in Medieval Thought and Learning: From Abelard to Wycliffe.* London: Hambledon Press, 1981.

Smith, Timothy L. *Thomas Aquinas' Trinitarian Theology.* Washington, D.C.: Catholic University of America Press, 2003.

Sommerfeldt, John R. *The Spiritual Teachings of Bernard of Clairvaux.* Kalamazoo, MI: Cistercian Publications, 1991.

Southern, R.W., ed. and trans. *The Life of St. Anselm, Archbishop of Canterbury, by Eadmer.* Oxford: Clarendon Press, 1962.

Southern, R.W. *St. Anselm: A Portrait in a Landscape.* Cambridge: Cambridge University Press, 1990.

Sweeney, Eileen C. *Anselm of Canterbury and the Desire for the Word.* Washington, D.C.: Catholic University of America Press, 2012.

Tamburello, Daniel E. *Bernard of Clairvaux: Essential Writings.* New York: Crossroad, 2000.

Thiselton, Anthony C. *New Horizons in Hermeneutics.* Grand Rapids, MI: Zondervan, 1992.

———. *Hermeneutics: An Introduction.* Grand Rapids, MI: Eerdmans, 2009.

Torjesen, Karen Jo. *Hermeneutical Procedure and Theological Method in Origen's Exegesis.* Berlin: Walter de Gruyter, 1986.

Van Fleteren, Frederick and Joseph C. Schnaubelt, eds. *Augustine: Biblical Exegete.* New York: Peter Lang Publishing, 2001.

Van Fleteren, Frederick; Joseph C. Schnaubelt; and Joseph Reino, eds. *Augustine: Mystic and Mystagogue.* New York, Peter Lang Publishing, 1994.

Vaughn, Sally N. *The Abbey of Bec and the Anglo-Norman State 1034-1136.* Suffolk, UK: Boydell Press, 1981.

———. *Archbishop Anselm 1093-1109: Bec Missionary, Canterbury Primate, Patriarch of Another World.* Burlington, VT: Ashgate, 2012.

Verbeke, Gerard, ed. *Aquinas and the Problems of his Time.* The Hague: Leuven University Press, 1976.

Visser, Sandra and Thomas Williams. *Anselm.* Oxford: Oxford University Press, 2009.

Ward, Benedicta. *Anselm of Canterbury: His Life and Legacy.* London: Society for Promoting Christian Knowledge, 2009.

Weinandy, Thomas G. *Aquinas on Scripture: An Introduction to his Biblical Commentaries.* London: T&T Clark International, 2005.

Weinandy, Thomas G., Daniel A. Keating, and John P. Yocum, eds. *Aquinas on Doctrine: A Critical Introduction.* London: T&T Clarke, 2004.

Wingren, Gustaf. *Theology in Conflict.* Philadelphia, Muhlenberg Press, 1958.

Other Works

Amerson, Nathan D. "What is Man? Discussion from Anselmian Discourse." Presented at the 2019 conference of the International Society for the Study of Medieval Theology (IGTM), Linz, Austria.

———. "Anselm Among the Normans: Spiritual Leader or Exile?" Presented at the 2019 conference of the Atlantic Medieval Society, Memorial University, St. Johns, Newfoundland, Canada.

Bruun, Mette B. "Bernard of Clairvaux and the Landscape of Salvation" in *A Companion to Bernard of Clairvaux*, ed. Brian Patrick McGuire, volume 25 of *Brill's Companions to the Christian Tradition.* Boston: Brill, 2011.

Day, Caleb. "St. Anselm of Canterbury's *Cur Deus Homo* in light of penal substitution atonement models." Final paper submitted for THEO60250, Introduction to Medieval Theology, University of Notre Dame, Fall 2014.

De Costa, Ricardo. "The Soul in Saint Bernard of Clairvaux's Mysticism." *Revista De Humanidades,* 17-18 (2008): 201-210.

Delicata, Nadia. "*Paideia tou Kyriou*: From Origen to Medieval Exegesis". *Didaskalia* 27 (2016): 31-64.

Faller, Paul. "Bernard of Clairvaux – A Spirituality of Love." Accessed from www.academia.edu, 08 March 2019.

Hoffman, Tobias. "Freedom Without Choice: Medieval Theories of the Essence of Freedom." In *The Cambridge Companion to Medieval Ethics*, ed. Thomas Williams, Cambridge: Cambridge University Press, 2019.

McDonough, Conor. "Christ as head of the Church in Calvin and Aquinas." Master's Thesis in Dogmatic Theology, Fribourg University, 2017.

Scruggs, Ryan. "The 'One Merciful Event': Thomas Merton on Anselm's Cur Deus Homo". *The Merton Annual,* 2017.

Sirilla, Michael G. "The Theological and Pastoral Purposes of Aquinas' Biblical Commentaries". *Biblica et Patristica Thoruniensia*, 10 (2017) 3: 375-387.

Spencer, Mark K. "Perceiving the Image of God in the Whole Human Person." *The St. Anselm Journal*, 13:2 (2018): 1-18.

Sternhagen, Dominic. "The Divine Ideas in North American Thomism." Licentiate Dissertation, Pontifical Athenaeum Regina Apostolorum, Sep 2014.

Studer, John. "On the Steps of Humility and Pride: Bernard of Clairvaux." Pontifical Athenaeum Regina Apostolorum, Jan 2018.

Tsevreni, Magdalini. "A Systematic Reading of *De Libertate Arbitrii*: The Ideas of Freedom and the Will of Saint Anselm." *A Review of Medieval Studies*, 2 (2014), 61-78.

Van Nieuwenhove, Rik. "St. Anselm and St. Thomas Aquinas on 'Satisfaction': or how Catholic and Protestant understandings of the Cross differ." *Angelicum*, 80 (2003), 159-176.

Ventureyra, Scott. "The Cosmological Argument and the Place of Contestation in Philosophical Discourse: from Plato and Aristotle to Contemporary Debates." *Maritain Studies,* Vol. XXXII (2016): 51-70.

Wildberg, Christian. "Neoplatonism." *The Stanford Encyclopedia of Philosophy* (Summer 2019 Edition), Edward N. Zalta (ed.), https://plato.stanford.edu/archives/sum2019/entries/neoplatonism.

Wise, Joshua. "Satisfying the Debt to God: A Synthetic reading of Anselm and the Responsibility of the Theologian." Paper presented to the American Academy of Religion Mid-Atlantic Region Conference, 2017.

Zachuber, Johannes. "Transcendence and Immanence" in Daniel Whistler, ed. *The Edinburgh Critical History of 19th Century Theology*. Edinburgh: Edinburgh University Press, 2018.

Made in the USA
Middletown, DE
19 July 2022